FINDING MY WORDS

A Ruthless Commitment to Healing Gently After Trauma

A MEMOIR

Mark M. McNear

Renown Publishing
www.renownpublishing.com

Finding My Words / Mark M. McNear
ISBN-13: 978-1-952602-84-9

Praise for *Finding My Words* by Mark M. McNear

In a social media world that glorifies perfection, it's refreshing to read a raw and vulnerable story about the parts of our lives we'd rather leave hidden. Mark does a fantastic job of being both raw and hopeful, authentic yet compassionate. This book is a must-read!

Pastor Tyler Minton, Lacey, Washington

The promise of *Finding My Words* is a beautiful one: shame will die when you're able to tell your story to safe people. When we begin our healing journey, we wonder if our story is too unique or broken to fully heal. Mark McNear found himself in a similar place, filled with deep shame for his behavior and also deeply ashamed of the trauma that marked his life. McNear's story will draw you in and disrupt, but it's written as an invitation for you to engage with your story, too. It shows us how the difficulties we face provide clues to the stories that most await healing.

Jay Stringer

Psychotherapist and author of *Unwanted: How Sexual Brokenness Reveals Our Way to Healing*

In *Finding My Words*, Mark McNear uses his own story to show us that the way toward wholeness is not around suffering, but through it. Although he makes appropriate use of existing trauma literature in this book, the story he tells is uniquely his own. He invites us to bear witness to how his childhood abuse led to

addiction and, ultimately, through it to a place of healing. One of the things in Dr. McNear's book for which I am most grateful is the recognition that healing is not a destination, but a lifelong journey of honestly sharing joys and sorrows with fellow travelers.
Jason Kanz, PhD, ABPP
Board Certified in Clinical Neuropsychology
Author of four books, including the recent *Letters to the Beloved*

A raw, honest look at the bonds that break us, the addictions that consume us, and the power of redemption that can only come from Jesus Christ.
Heather Bedford, MEd, MA, LPC, NCC
Columbia, South Carolina

I've known Mark McNear for over forty years and have witnessed firsthand the transformative work of God's grace in his life, which he shares with such great vulnerability in this memoir. I also know firsthand that his deepest desire is for this book to help each reader embrace the reality of his or her own trauma with the overarching reality of God's ability to heal, restore, and redeem even the most painful life experiences. I pray that you'll be blessed, encouraged, and empowered in your own journey as Mark comes alongside you in sharing his own and that the path forward for you is paved with sturdy hope.
Pastor Bruce Hoppe
Christ Community Church, Greeley, Colorado

Dr. McNear shares his story with raw vulnerability. To face the agony of trauma and addiction but come out on the other side with such compassion and hope is inspiring. There really is hope to heal!

A must-read for those struggling with trauma, abuse, and or addiction.
Jonathan Wiggins
Lead Pastor of Rez.Church, Loveland, Colorado
Author of *Walking with Lions*

Mark has answered the high call and walked a journey that took him to a healed heart. This story is incredible, an amazing example of God's redemptive love. You might ask yourself how on earth such deep trauma could *ever* find transformation into a gateway of hope. You don't want to miss this masterpiece!
Heather Lines-Degelman, APNC-RN
Succasunna, New Jersey

Working with Mark, I would never have believed he endured such trauma and abuse. His ability to connect, relate, and bring humor to our clients was remarkable. His life story is a testament to Hebrews 2:4: "And God confirmed the message by giving signs and wonders and various miracles" (NLT). I believe the power of God through his story will heal, save, and deliver many!
Kathleen Kohaut
Certified Alcohol and Drug Counselor
BS Addiction Studies
Leland, North Carolina

At the root of addiction lies trauma; we know this as therapists and survivors. But, how exactly does one find healing on the other side of complex childhood trauma? *Finding My Words* is a rare blend of profoundly personal narrative infused with professional insights regarding the dynamics of trauma and addiction gleaned from Dr. Mark McNear's many years as a therapist. Mark shows us what it looks like to move through the recovery process from a first-person

perspective, demystifying trauma and addiction recovery. Mark offers a window into his first memories as a young boy and the impact of childhood trauma that often goes on behind closed doors, even in families who hold a positive reputation within the community. Mark walks the reader through his process of "defragging" his complex trauma narrative as he finds the words to talk about what happened and reframe his sense of self-worth.
Jennifer Wilson Loggins, M.S. LPC CPCS
Adjunct Instructor of Psychology, Brenau University
Gainesville, Georgia

It has been said that if we don't transform our pain, we will certainly transmit it. Mark McNear shows us in this wonderful book that the opposite is also true: if we do transform our pain, we can pass on healing, wisdom, and grace to others. McNear, a professional helper, turns his pen on the pain, complexity, and beauty of his own story in a way that will capture your heart. He speaks with deep honesty about his trauma, but also about his recovery by the grace of God. Whether you are attempting to face your own trauma story or help someone around you do the same, I believe Mark's story will be a gift and an encouragement to you.
Nick Stumbo
Executive Director
Pure Desire Ministries, Troutdale, Oregon

This book is a must for all ministry leaders helping broken people find healing in the gospel. My wife and I were both broken and encouraged by reading Mark's story. His transparent honesty will bring hope to those struggling with hidden pain and will give

insight to family and friends as they journey together toward healing and restoration.
Pastor Doug Thuen
Sparta Evangelical Free Church, Sparta, New Jersey

In *Finding My Words,* Mark courageously and vulnerably shares his journey through abuse, trauma, lies, and addictions. This book will bring God's hope and answers to your life, regardless of the pain and struggles you have experienced.
Ben Bennett
Speaker and author, Josh McDowell Ministry
Director of Resolution Movement

One of the most soul-crushing aspects of the abuse of a child is the conviction that the child is bad and that the abuse is to be kept a secret to not expose the child's "evil." The belief is that exposure to light opens secrecy and misinformation to hard examination. It is all too frequent that children subjected to abuse(s) are cowed by secrecy and the "gaslighting" that they deserve their pain when, actually, it is the fault of the adult who abuses them.

In *Finding My Words*, Dr. Mark McNear graphically pulls away the scars in eloquently exposing the depths and residuals of childhood abuse in all the forms it was experienced. He clearly depicts the emotional pain that superseded the physical and sexual abuse. Dr. McNear bravely narrates his obstacle-filled past to shine a brilliant sun on the truth of his experiences.

An analyst once requoted, "Living well is the best revenge," but it is Dr. McNear's account of his process of healing that demonstrates empathy for all in his situation, inclusive of himself. He has worked around revenge.

Celeste A. Jacque, MD
Diplomate, American Board of Child & Adolescent Psychology
Diplomate, American Board of Psychiatry & Neurology

To Debbie, Emily, and Brandon.

And to everyone who has followed and assisted me on my journey.

CONTENTS

A Cautionary Note to Readers

GRAPHIC CONTENT WARNING

Some of the content in this book shares graphic descriptions of child abuse. It has the propensity to trigger people who have struggled with child abuse, trauma, or addiction.

If this describes you, the reader, I encourage you to put the book down and find someone experienced in child abuse, trauma, or addiction recovery to read this book with you, rather than reading it alone.

If you have been abused or are being abused, please reach out to an abuse hotline. If you're in the U. S., please contact the National Sexual Assault Hotline by calling 800.656.HOPE (4673) or via online chat at https://hotline.rainn.org/online. They will assist you on your path to freedom.

Foreword by Josh McDowell

Mark McNear's story is important.

How do I know this? You see, Mark's story, in many ways, is my story. It's a story that no doubt has been experienced by thousands, even millions, across the globe. And, dare I say, it may be your story as well.

What should be a safe place for children—home and family—I found to be a frightening and even dangerous space. I grew up in a dysfunctional family with an alcoholic, violent father and a sexually abusive caregiver. This caused tremendous problems in my life and fueled the fire of anger as I buried my family secrets deep in my heart.

Mark, like many childhood survivors of abuse and trauma, buried his wounds and memories while pouring himself into his education and eventual work as a licensed psychotherapist. He was a successful man with a wonderful wife and beautiful daughter.

But Mark's childhood story caught up with him. And suddenly, as the bottom dropped out of his life, Mark recognized that the only way out was to look up. God was closer than Mark had realized. With God by his side, it was time for him to stop running away from his childhood. Instead, surrounded by caring, safe people and professionals, it was time to face it.

Maybe as you are reading this, you can relate to that concept of running away: running from your addiction, from your abuse, from your trauma—and from God.

As a child, I went to church and prayed, even in the chaos of my home life. But my anger not only buried my trauma, it buried my belief in God as well. As a young man, I considered myself agnostic. I honestly believed that Christianity was worthless. However, while in college, when challenged to examine the claims of Christianity intellectually, I discovered compelling, overwhelming evidence for the reliability of the Christian faith.

Once I trusted in Jesus Christ as Savior and Lord, my life changed dramatically as I experienced the power of God's love. And like Mark, I was able to start facing the trauma of my childhood and find healing.

In reading Mark's book, many things stood out to me, but what really struck me was that Mark embraced God's unconditional acceptance of him—right in the middle of his horrible mess. He says that God's grace "was like a bright light shining in my murky world. I could be a broken, wounded, and sinful person, yet still be loved by God and treated tenderly and kindly by Him. I have seen His grace throughout this tiring process time and again."

Mark's experience is my experience. Though my childhood trauma and abuse left me with a lifetime of scars, it also did something else: it brought me to the God who loves me. And that changed my life and brought healing beyond measure.

Whether you have experienced trauma, abuse, addiction, or any other horrible situation in your life that robbed you of peace and altered your story, please know that your life can be different. There are new chapters to write—ones that include healing, recovery, peace, and joy.

Friend, your story is still being written. Your life does not have to be dictated by your trauma. In fact, God promises those who grieve that He will "bestow on them a crown of beauty instead of ashes, the oil of joy instead of mourning, and a garment of praise instead of a spirit of despair. They will be called oaks of righteousness, a planting of the LORD for the display of his splendor" (Isaiah 61:3).

Does this all sound too good to be true? It's not. Whatever you're going through, God has seen others, like Mark and me, through similar trauma. If God can do it for them and us, He can do it for you now.

That's why this book is so important! Trauma, abuse, and addiction do not own your story. Read on, through Mark's book. You will see by the end that Mark McNear's story is one of hope, forgiveness, and abundant grace.

Yes, that's Josh McDowell's story, too. And it can be yours as well.

Josh McDowell, author and speaker
Josh McDowell Ministry

INTRODUCTION

A Bright Light in a Murky World

As I sit here at my desk, it is seven years ago to the day that I walked through the doors of the Caron Treatment Center and checked myself into rehab. Never in my wildest dreams would I ever have thought I would one day be writing an introduction to a book sharing some of my childhood trauma. (What I've included is not the totality, but just a glimpse of my life's story.) The trauma led to a troubled life, which blossomed into addictions and maladaptive behaviors.

There were countless times in the past when I wrestled with God. I would tell Him I would not revisit my childhood and would definitely not write down any incidents that happened. I would never share those things with anyone. But as you can see, God had other plans and won that wrestling match.

This book has been sixty-plus years in the making, yet it was finally birthed at a Friday-night dinner with a couple I respect, admire, and love. In this safe and intimate setting, I shared parts of my life's story. They challenged me to write it down as a memoir, both for myself and as a message of hope to others struggling with their traumas and addictions.

While writing this book has often been a challenging process—going through the emotional toll of revisiting traumas, facing the reality of my addictions, and recounting the negative impact they have had on me and others—I believe it has all been worth it. I wrote this for those struggling with trauma, addictions, or mental health issues. It can also give insight to those desperately trying to support a loved one or a friend who is on a course of self-inflicted destruction. It will help them more clearly understand what that individual is dealing with and that recovery is a multifaceted, ongoing process.

There is hope. I can look back on the immense pain and this long journey to see it has led to an incomprehensible victory. Throughout rehab and then later in recovery, I experienced God's grace in big and small ways. I learned that grace, which is God's unmerited favor toward us, is the ultimate act of love. God's unconditional acceptance of me, right in the middle of my horrible mess, was like a bright light shining in my murky world. I could be a broken, wounded, and sinful person, yet still be loved by God and treated tenderly and kindly by Him. I have seen His grace throughout this tiring process time and again.

I have been asked by some people who know me if I see myself as an adult child of an alcoholic, as an addict, as someone dealing with PTSD or complex trauma, etc. My response is that while labels may be helpful for some things, they don't describe the whole person. Besides, labels are for soup cans and not people! I prefer to recognize myself as beloved of God.

To sum all this up, I'll end with a passage from Brennan Manning's book *The Ragamuffin Gospel*: "When I get honest, I admit I am a bundle of paradoxes. I believe and I doubt, I hope and I get discouraged, I love and I hate, I feel bad about feeling good, I feel guilty about not feeling guilty. I am trusting and suspicious. I am honest and I still play games. Aristotle said I am a rational animal; I say I am an angel with an incredible capacity for beer. To live by grace means acknowledging my whole life story, the light side and the dark."[1]

I can so relate to Mr. Manning. I pray my journey from darkness to light will point others to hope and freedom.

Mark M. McNear
March 2022

Part A: Rehab

CHAPTER ONE

Trying to Outrun My Memories and Emotions

> As long as you keep secrets and suppress information, you are fundamentally at war with yourself.... The critical issue is allowing yourself to know what you know. That takes an enormous amount of courage.[2]
>
> **—Bessel van der Kolk, MD**

I walked through the doors, and my heart sank. I had no idea what to expect next. This was clearly not something I wanted to add to my resume. It scared me. How did I—a healthcare professional, a therapist, a Christian, and a man who helps others with their difficulties—let this happen?

Just being there reaffirmed I was a loser, a failure, and a fool. I had lied to myself and others, and I had let my life get out of control.

I looked over at my wife, Debbie, who smiled reassuringly at me. I knew I had disappointed her and my daughter, Emily. I had disappointed my family, friends, and clients. Most importantly, I felt I had deeply disappointed God.

While I waited for the intake process to begin, I experienced deep despair. In one sense, I felt like my life was over. This feeling also confirmed the message my dad had given me for years: there was something wrong with me. Still, deep inside me, there was a tiny glimmer of hope for change.

Three Reasons I Entered Rehab

What led me to enter rehab? To put it simply, I wasn't functioning well. I wasn't able to leave the house. I lay in bed for at least half of the day and avoided taking part in life for the rest. I was in bad shape. I was depressed, had mood swings, was emotionally abusive, and could not provide for my family. I had created a chaotic home life for my wife and my daughter—so much so that Emily moved to Florida at a young age. She gave other reasons for moving, but I knew she was escaping the mess I had caused in our home. I really couldn't blame her. I knew what it was like growing up in such a family.

Richard Rohr says, "If we don't transform our pain, we most assuredly will transmit it."[3] There I was in my fifties, creating an environment similar, in some ways, to the one I had hated living in.

I would really like to say I recognized my problem and that is what led me to enter rehab, but it took more than that. There were three pivotal reasons I entered rehab and changed the trajectory of my life.

The first reason was that my addictions were exposed. I

was taking numerous prescriptions and had been for three decades, but I found myself in a place where my refills and prescriptions ran out. I was trying to manipulate things to get the medication, knowing it was an uphill climb because I was taking way too much. When you take next week's medication today, you come up short—quickly.

I had called the doctor, asking her for refills on my medications, and it soon became apparent to her that I was abusing the medications. Right away, without any hesitation, she recommended I go to rehab because I had a problem and needed help. She didn't mince words. Though I was taken aback, I eventually came to realize this was, indeed, a divine appointment.

The second reason was that my family agreed I needed rehab. After speaking to the doctor, I knew I had to talk to my wife. I told her what the doctor said about me abusing my prescription medications and needing to go to rehab. Debbie completely agreed with the doctor. It was apparent to her that I had a serious problem. I then texted my daughter in Florida, and the response I got from her, yet again, was she knew I had a problem. Like my wife, Emily was not surprised. Later, I realized our interactions pointed to this truth: nearly everyone sees the addiction, except the addict.

Both my wife and daughter were very supportive. Their response to my addictions was tremendously impactful for me. They showed such compassion and grace. They knew I had a problem and needed to get help, but they undergirded their words and actions with tremendous love; they wanted to see me get better. This was a huge boost to me in seeking the help I needed. It gave me the resolve I needed to change.

The third reason for me to enter rehab was that my dad had passed away eight months prior. At first glance, it may seem strange that my dad's passing had anything to do with me deciding to go to rehab. However, for me, it was a sign that the coast was clear and I could finally deal with the tribulations and pain of my childhood. I didn't have to hide anything anymore. I didn't have to worry about the next part of my life, and I could find the healing I longed for after all those years. It was the last barrier that came down to allow me to address my addictions and the deeper pain that had resided in my heart from my childhood.

PREPARING FOR REHAB

With the doctor, Debbie, and Emily encouraging me to go to rehab, I began to research facilities around the country. I also talked to my fellow mental-health professionals, who recommended the Caron Treatment Center in Wernersville, Pennsylvania. I concluded I needed inpatient rehab. I needed to get away and focus one hundred percent on my recovery and healing.

I started the intake process over the phone and made some financial arrangements. Amid the paperwork I had to fax to the facility was a sheet on which I described what I was being treated for. I wrote, "I have a whole bushel basket full of mental health diagnoses and a lot of chronic pain." It was an honest assessment.

Though I had not worked much for the past four months,

my clients were called and informed that I wouldn't be seeing patients for a while. I put on my voicemail that I would be out of the office for an extended period for health reasons. Little did I know that it would be over two years before I returned to work even part-time.

Finding My Courage: The First Day of Rehab

Since I had discontinued medication and was going through withdrawal, some of what I remember happening is a bit blurry. One thing I remember clearly was the weather. On that day in March of 2015 when Debbie and I drove out to the Caron Treatment Center in Pennsylvania, it was a beautiful, sunny day. It was a long drive from our house to the facility. Seeing as I was in no shape to drive, Debbie drove, and I tried to sit back and relax. I have to say that it was a peaceful and scenic trip, with farms and farmland dotting the route most of the way. At first, I was quiet and subdued. Eventually, we had a good conversation that was very hopeful about our future. Deep down inside, however, I felt like I had failed and that my life was over.

My heart pounded when we drove up to the facility. Any peaceful feeling I had experienced on the drive quickly faded when I entered the doors of the Caron Treatment Center. I was glad the place seemed warm and inviting. The staff ushered me into one room and Debbie into another. I would be meeting with the intake administrator while Debbie met with the counselor who would be working with me.

The rooms seemed rather sterile and bland, with little to no decorations. I sat down in front of the desk with the intake administrator, who was busily typing on the computer. Even with the paperwork I had already faxed over to the facility, she had me sign what seemed like a million more forms, many having to do with consent. As she continued giving me the screen to sign the forms electronically, I told her how hard this whole process was for me. She kindly and gently affirmed what I said, nodded, and responded, "I know it is."

Besides the process itself, it was nerve-racking to hear Debbie and the counselor talking in the other room and not being able to make out what they were saying. I remember thinking, *"This isn't good."*

Next, I was escorted into another room with a couple of chairs to meet with the intake clinician. The person asked me more about my history. I gave details regarding the medications I had been taking and my abuse of them. I also touched upon my childhood abuse, something I had never talked about with anyone. As I shared certain aspects of my abuse, I started crying. My crying turned into sobs, which turned into uncontrollable weeping. I think it was the most I had ever cried, at least as an adult.

After my interviews with the clinician and the counselor, I think I might have undergone a physical exam. However, I'm not exactly sure that's the way it happened. Like I mentioned, my memory of certain aspects of my rehab is fuzzy. Regardless, it was determined I didn't need detox, which spared me from being in another part of the facility with increased medical attention. One aspect of this process stands out to me: it's peculiar how quickly I got used to other people making decisions for me, seeing as I'd only been there a few hours.

I finally was taken to the floor where I would be staying for the next twenty-eight days. I was assigned to both group therapy sessions, which occurred daily, and individual therapy, which occurred several times a week. Before going and meeting the other people I would be staying with, the counseling assistants took me to my room.

I was glad to see that my room didn't look or have the feel of a hospital room. It had one large bed, a closet, and a bathroom with a shower. My two escorts proceeded to go through every single item in my luggage to make sure I had not brought any "contraband" with me. I felt a great level of shame and humiliation that this was what my life had come to in my mid-fifties.

Though I was feeling tired, I was next introduced to the staff and other patients on my floor. I was surprised to learn some of the patients were healthcare professionals like myself—dentists, pharmacists, anesthesiologists, and such. It was helpful for me to meet them and know there were other professionals who had the same struggles I did. It eased some of my shame and built a bond I never dreamed I would find at a rehab facility.

I was ambivalent when I got back to my room. It had been a long, excruciatingly painful day. It was about 11 p.m., and I was exhausted. Yet, when I lay down on the bed, sleep evaded me. I just stared at the blinking red light of the smoke detector above my bed. I recall asking myself, *"How on earth did I end up here?"* My mind was awash with thoughts and feelings. I felt like I was never going to be normal again. I had spent more than thirty years trying to outrun my memories of childhood, but it seemed like I had lost that race.

As tears welled up in my eyes once again, I suddenly remembered the verse Debbie had given me earlier in the day: "Weeping may endure for a night, but joy comes in the morning" (Psalm 30:5 NKJV).

HEALING TAKES LONGER THAN TWENTY-EIGHT DAYS

Considering that for years I had used prescription medications to regulate my mood and help me to sleep, it was a huge adjustment getting used to my new schedule. The only time spent in my room was for sleeping. The rest of my day and evening was spent with other people, which was uncomfortable. Since I wasn't used to being around that many people, in the first few weeks I was there, the staff allowed me to take a few short naps on some days. Getting acclimated to a regular schedule, including regular eating and sleeping routines, wasn't easy at first, but it was crucial to my healing.

After several weeks in the program, I ended up enjoying being around other people all day, but I certainly did not initially. I was withdrawn during the first few weeks in rehab. I would sit with my arms crossed in front of my chest at all my group meetings. In a sense, I was trying to protect myself from this new world I was inhabiting.

There were many, many meetings. The group sessions were in a room with chairs spread out to form a circle. While the others shared about their struggles, I mostly listened. It was in those meetings that we did our Twelve-Step work. It was structured to help us step out of denial, talk about our usage, and understand the powerlessness we felt in our addictions. I honestly felt overwhelmed. Though everyone was very friendly, it took me several weeks to warm up to it all and start participating a little.

WHEN BAD MEMORIES CATCH UP WITH YOU

The pain got much worse before it got better. As the medications were leaving my body, I was going through withdrawal both physically and emotionally. I began to connect with some of the other patients, but I didn't share anything about my trauma. Thankfully, for the first time in many years, I had brief moments of time when I could tolerate the experience of emotions in my body.

As the medications went out of my system, the memories started coming back strong. The emotions hit me like a tidal wave, and my body tightened up. It was as if I were reliving my abusive childhood. I felt a surge of hormones as my body's fight, flight, freeze, or fawn reactions kicked in. My head and my body were filled with bad memories. Ironically, what made it worse was my natural propensity to block my experience of emotions, which is common for people who have suffered trauma. Instead of providing relief, it just made what I was thinking and feeling more painful.

One of the main places people experience trauma is in their bodies. You feel uptight, dizzy, and numb. You shut down one moment and experience panic the next. The feelings of danger consume you. You can think about something that happened years ago, and you experience it in your body today. That's what started happening to me in rehab. I experienced profound emotional dysregulation. As the thoughts and memories started flooding my mind, I felt the impact in my body.

Memories of my childhood abuse came back vividly. As horrible as it was, it helped me to realize I had become addicted to medications because I wanted to numb the pain. I took the medications (and then some) because I didn't want to think about or emotionally experience my childhood trauma. It took so much energy in my life to try not to think about these things.

For most of my time in rehab, I worked on not thinking about the memories, trying to block them any way I could. But that didn't work. The people around me were gently encouraging me and permitting me to think about my childhood and how I felt, while I was saying to myself, *"No, no, no, I'm not going there. I can't go there!"*

We were all encouraged to open up and start telling our stories, but I kept saying to myself, *"No way. I will never tell my story. My story is too big for me to tell, even to myself. I don't feel safe."*

Deep down, I knew God wanted to get this stuff out of me. The wounds of my abuse and the memories that debilitated me were not things God wanted me to carry. Instead, God wanted me to give these things to Him and allow Him to carry them, and one of the ways He does this is through other people!

At the end of each of our group meetings, we would put our arms around each other and say the Serenity Prayer: "God grant me the serenity to accept the things that I cannot change, the courage to change the things that I can, and the wisdom to know the difference." This was wisdom I desperately needed. The whole experience was a tremendous time of bonding and healing for me.

During my time in rehab, I found great encouragement in my meetings with the psychiatrist, Dr. Joseph Garbley. Just thinking about our interactions makes me smile. He was informed, kind, compassionate, and gentle. I experienced him as safe. He shared some of his story with me, including that he'd had trauma and addiction in his life. He told me it was going to take time to heal. I needed to hear that, that I could take time to heal.

Safe people are not judging you, rolling their eyes, or shaking their heads at you. They aren't gasping or saying you shouldn't feel this way or that way. Instead, they let you speak freely, allowing the difficult things to come to the surface. It's a big part of the healing journey.

When I first entered rehab, I expected to be there for twenty-eight days, but a few weeks into my stay, the staff recommended I go to extended care. My first reaction was intense anger. I went into rehab in denial and thinking this whole process was very cut and dried. I figured I would just get this done and be out of there.

But as I started walking the pathway toward healing, I realized how much work needed to be done. I was grateful I didn't have to rush the process. As I stepped back, I found great comfort in knowing I didn't have to fix everything quickly. My journey would be long.

Yes, my first few weeks in rehab were a whirlwind of emotions and pain, but it was also the first time in my life that I saw a glimpse of freedom and the beginning of healing. When I entered rehab, I was convinced God was done with me. But He wasn't, not at all. God showed up at the Caron Treatment Center. He was right by my side in the darkest parts of my story, offering light, truth, mercy, and grace—though, I admit, it was very hard to see at the time through the pain I was experiencing.

Chapter One Reflections

Question: Do you have any behaviors in your life you are hesitant to give up, behaviors that take up too much time, cause harm, or have other negative consequences?

____

____

____

____

____

____

____

____

____

Question: What circumstances, experiences, or behaviors of yours have brought you a sense of guilt, shame, or humiliation? Have you been able to share them with anyone? Have you shared them with God? If so, how?

Question: Has there ever been something in your life you avoided dealing with? What was the result? Did you ever get to the point where you could face it? If not, what might it take for you to address that issue?

Chapter One Notes

CHAPTER TWO

When You Can't Find the Words

The question is not why the addiction, but why the pain.[4]

—Dr. Gabor Maté

I was exhausted. The group meeting went long, and it was good to be back in my room, alone. But sleep was escaping me. I stared at the ceiling, thinking about the group conversation. It was true that the real problem was not the addiction. I needed to address the harder questions: What was driving the addiction? What pain was I trying to medicate?

I was gradually learning that the problem wasn't so much my addiction to prescription drugs, but the pain I was carrying. I let the tears drip slowly down my face. Rehab was hard. It was painful. Deep down, I knew my addictions were misguided attempts to deal with the real problem, which was the complex trauma I experienced when I was a child.

I said a prayer: "Lord, please help me."

I slept fitfully but was thankful that Jesus showed up in the mess.

UNMASKING THE PROBLEM

My real problem was not the addiction to prescription drugs. The addiction certainly caused issues in my life, but it served as my mask, hiding the pain of my troubling childhood. If I didn't deal with the source of my pain, ten other addictions might crop up.

Addictions in people aren't happenstance. They are there for a reason. They are a means of escaping or avoiding the tremendous pain and trauma people suffer, as well as the life-changing experiences people have.

After two to three weeks in rehab, my mask started crumbling, and I was in intense pain. Thoughts I had previously shut down by medicating myself started to come alive. I had no medications or vices to combat the unwanted memories. I was helpless.

I can't tell you how much despair, anxiety, and confusion I experienced in those first few weeks of rehab. I was bombarded with thoughts of my childhood and its pain, and I wanted to block them out. That's what I had done my whole life, shut them out. But now, my mask was being ripped away, and I felt helpless to the process.

One morning, I woke up to a full-fledged panic attack. I was at the sink in my bathroom, getting ready for the day, and I felt intense emotional and physical pain. I was dizzy and had an ocular migraine, which caused spots in my vision. I was paralyzed by feelings of fear and dread. I made it to my bed to sit down and started taking deep breaths. I kept thinking, *"I've got to get through this. I've got to make it to breakfast."*

That experience, as difficult as it was, is a good illustration of the recovery process. Sometimes you just need to do the next thing and get through it, rather than overthinking or trying to grasp the entire process at one time. Focusing on doing the next thing helped me to get through each hour, each day, and each week. The rehab process was extensive, structured, and busy. There was no time to hang out in your room or watch TV. (I think we were allowed to watch one hour of news every morning).

My days and weeks were filled with lectures and counseling sessions. I had basic care management counseling that organized my schedule and life while also determining when Debbie would visit. I had group counseling sessions that addressed the Steps Program for overcoming addiction and another session that addressed "our stories" to help us deal with the problems we were desperately trying to escape through our addictions. I also had one-on-one sessions with a psychologist who started to do basic trauma work with me regarding my childhood. Though my schedule was intense, I also found it to be immensely helpful. This process that was causing so much pain and anxiety was the very process I needed in order to face the wounds of my childhood.

Taking Me Where I Did Not Want to Go

It's hard to face the pain trauma causes and even harder when you're doing it alone. Rehab was set up in such a way as to limit one's time alone. My schedule was structured and busy. Except for one-on-one counseling sessions and going to bed to sleep, I was continually around people. Whether it was classes, group sessions, meals, or breaks, for the most part, no one was allowed to isolate.

Like everything with rehab and recovery, the path to healing was confronting the very problem I had spent years trying to escape. I no longer had my medications, and my mask for hiding my trauma was being peeled away painfully. In the one-on-one and group counseling sessions, the pain of my childhood, which I had vowed as a little kid never to talk about and had tucked away securely, was seeping out and slowly flooding my mind and my body.

It was like a wrestling match going on in my head. On one hand, the thoughts and feelings of the abuse I experienced as a child were coming forward. On the other hand, I was doing everything I could to suppress them while trying to act normal in rehab!

Group sessions were particularly difficult for me. Everyone at rehab had a story to tell about the real problem and pain behind his addiction. As person after person shared his story, thinking about sharing mine still felt too big for me emotionally. How could I talk about something I didn't even have the words to express? I simply wasn't able to do it. I didn't yet feel safe enough to share the story of my childhood, let alone the abuse, in a group setting.

As I listened to others' stories, thoughts about my childhood would surface, but I would shut them down, withdrawing into myself. One of the hardest parts of processing it all was the reality that the past isn't the past when it's coming up in the present. As I attempted to block my thoughts of childhood events, they came back with even more energy.

Memories of my childhood and flashbacks to that time were activated in my mind, and I felt them both emotionally and physically. The fear, anger, and dread that came from reliving my abuse manifested in my body through anxiety, panic attacks, stomach pain, headaches, and other ailments. My way to deal with it all was to withdraw.

I was living a dichotomy. I was committed to getting better, but I was against doing what it would take to get better. I was not willing to go through my childhood again. No way was I going to face that pain. Such ambivalence! This battle became tiring for my mind and my body. I thought I could figure out a different way to heal.

JESUS SHOWS UP IN MY MESS

Though I knew God was with me in this process, I also felt I had done too much damage to our relationship to experience His grace and mercy. But Jesus continued to be at my side. He was faithful. His grace and mercy toward me were not dependent on my feelings. That was something, as a Christian, I needed to learn and embrace.

While I was struggling with the process of facing the damage from my childhood, desperately wanting to find a different path toward healing, Jesus showed up in a big way. After another long day in rehab, I was finally back in my room and getting ready for bed. Once I lay down, I began to think about verses of Scripture. One that came to mind was John 5:6. Jesus had come across a man who was paralyzed. The verse says, "When Jesus saw him lying there and learned that he had been in this condition for a long time, he asked him, 'Do you want to get well?'" (John 5:6).

It was as if Jesus were right there in my room, looking at me with compassion, and asking, "Mark, do you want to get well?"

I would like to be able to say I knew, without a doubt, that there was no other way to find healing than to confront my past instead of running from it. But to be honest, I wrestled with this not just for months, but for years! Did I want to continue going through the pain of the process? No, not at all. However, I did want to get well. Though I knew I had a long journey ahead of me, I also knew Jesus would be with me on this very messy path to healing. My whole reason for wanting to get better was because of my relationship with God and my relationships with Debbie and Emily, my family.

Each day at rehab, I was confronted with the fact that I had to address both the addictions and the trauma. In the midst of the process, my heart opened to the crucial idea of exploring my story with kindness and curiosity rather than judgment. It was a model Jesus demonstrated throughout His ministry on earth.

Another important attribute Jesus demonstrated toward people was compassion. Since I didn't see compassion modeled while I was growing up, I had to learn from other people and, of course, from Jesus' example. Just as I knew I shouldn't judge other people because of their stories, I had to learn not to judge myself. Rather than taking a sledgehammer to my story and beating myself up, I needed to enter my story with kindness, compassion, and curiosity.

Romans 2:4 says, "Or do you have contempt for the wealth of his kindness, forbearance, and patience, and yet do not know that God's kindness leads you to repentance?" (NET). God's kindness, combined with His "wealth" of tolerance and patience, drew me in. He walked with me through the messiness of facing my story, and He is still walking with me today. Since there is no condemnation for those who are in Christ (Romans 8:1), there is no reason for me to feel condemned or to give credence to self-condemnation.

Too often in rehab, I found I was extremely critical of my struggles and failings. I would think and sometimes say things such as: *"How did I end up here? What's the matter with me? Why am I such a fool?"*

On this journey, I was encouraged to stop critiquing my thoughts and behaviors and instead to begin the process of assessment. When I assess what is, I'm looking at the things in my life that need change and adjustment from a position of kindness, forgiveness, and grace. This approach brings life rather than death.

After the first three weeks, I was starting to feel better and getting to know other people. I was even building friendships. Then, one day, a group of us were in the hall, kidding around about something and laughing. It felt great to laugh and have fun. One of the older therapists walked down the hallway and looked at us. My friends smiled and kept on having a fun time, but I froze. Immediately, I was brought back to my childhood and my dad not allowing me to have fun. Though I was making some progress and building relationships and trust, it was obvious that the triggers of my childhood were very much in play and my path to healing would be more complicated than I had ever imagined.

Addressing My Addictions

My addiction to prescriptions started when I was about twenty-eight and lasted into my mid-fifties. The addiction not only affected me individually, but also had profound effects on my family. The fact that I wasn't able to be there for my wife and daughter in the way I should still fills me with deep sadness and remorse.

Just as I had individual sessions to deal with the root pain behind my addictions, my childhood trauma, I also had group counseling sessions to address the addictions. These group sessions, which had two counselors, helped us to work through the Twelve-Step Program. I was given both the Narcotics Anonymous book and the Alcoholics Anonymous book (also called The Big Book). The steps resonated with me, especially when discussing denial and powerlessness. In later steps, you look at where your life is and where you want it to be. Another crucial step is realizing only a power greater than yourself can restore you to sanity.

Deception, including self-deception, was a big problem in my life. At an incredibly early age, I learned how to lie and to manipulate. Whenever my dad would ask a question, I would pause, afraid, and stare at him while running various scenarios through my head to find the best (or safest) answer to give him. Since I suffered great abuse at the hands of my father, my lying became a survival mechanism from as early in childhood as I can remember. What would be the best answer to give him? What answer would appease him and bring me some sort of escape or relief?

My pattern of lying continued throughout my life until I entered rehab. During the moral inventories that took place in counseling, I was able to realize and acknowledge the deception and self-deception that had been prominent in my childhood and adulthood.

Another important factor that coincided with my addictions was my inability to self-regulate. It was extremely hard for me to regulate myself emotionally. I'm not sure I had ever really done so in my life. Most people learn to self-regulate through their parents' teaching and examples. Considering my childhood, it was obvious why I never really learned or found effective ways to manage my emotions.

Researchers have found that when people get together with others, it helps them to regulate emotionally. That's why a big part of recovery programs is having people working together in groups. It not only builds self-regulation skills, but also provides for transparency and accountability. Scripture talks about the benefit of coming together with others to help and encourage one another, confess your sins to each other, and build one another up. We are not meant to walk alone in life.

One of the things I noticed early in the Twelve-Step Program was the lesson not to tell or promise my family, friends, co-workers, or others that I'm going to change, but to *show them*. I really took that to heart, and it became a motto for me. I had already caused others a great deal of pain, and I didn't want to promise them I'd change without actually doing it. One thing I knew for sure: I was motivated to change and find the healing in my life that I so desperately needed.

THE NEWS I DIDN'T WANT TO HEAR

When I entered rehab, it was understood I would stay for around thirty days. As I mentioned earlier, when I came near the expected end date, I was brought into a meeting with my counselors and administrators. It was then that they recommended I stay for another two months, in another part of the facility, to pursue a higher level of therapy. Debbie and Emily were at the rehab facility that day as well. Initially, I fought the counselors' recommendation tooth and nail.

Debbie and Emily went to lunch with me to talk about the extended stay. It was a huge deciding point in my life. I had been looking forward to going home, so the thought of staying at the rehab facility for another two months, with more-extensive therapy regarding my trauma, was not something I initially could conceive of doing. But with immense compassion and love, Debbie and Emily challenged me to accept the recommendation that I needed to continue my journey toward healing. I decided to stay another two months at rehab. Though I didn't see it at the time, it was one of the best things I've ever done in my life.

Chapter Two Reflections

Question: Are you running from something in your past? If so, why do you think you are avoiding it?

____

____

____

____

____

____

____

____

____

____

Question: Do you want to get well? What would it look like for you to get well?

Question: In what ways is the pain from your past hindering you from living fully today?

___

___

___

___

___

___

___

___

___

___

___

___

Chapter Two Notes

CHAPTER THREE

Feeling Safe in My Own Skin

> Trauma survivors need to be safe in order to heal; they need to feel some sense of control over their lives now; they do not need to feel small or less than others or ashamed.[5]
>
> **—Janina Fisher, PhD**

I sat outside, enjoying the beautiful day and the scenic landscape of the rehabilitation facility, with its open fields, green grass, gardens, and Adirondack chairs sprinkled throughout. Of course, I had thought I would be out of rehab and home after thirty days, but here I was in what they called "extended care," diving more deeply into my healing journey and the feelings that emerged with it.

That morning's group session was exhausting but helpful. There was no doubt I struggled with shame and guilt. I sat looking at the serene view in front of me, and I couldn't help but long for serenity in my heart and mind.

The Guilt and Shame of My Childhood Trauma

I felt a great deal of guilt and shame in my life and wrestled quite a bit with both. Much of it came from my childhood abuse and the immense pain that ensued, but I also felt guilt and shame from my addictions and how they impacted my family and my friends, as well as my career.

Guilt and shame seem to dissipate when you're able to tell your story to safe people. Though I struggled with both intense feelings, I also had a tremendous resolve to get better and a resilience that believed I could heal. Granted, I didn't know how I would get better, but I did have the determination to heal.

When my counselor told me trauma survivors need to feel safe to heal and need to feel some sense of control over our lives, it resonated with me. The trauma I experienced stripped me of having any control over my well-being. The very person who should have been my protector, my father, was instead my abuser. My home, which should have been a safe place for me to run to, was instead the place where danger lurked. I had come to realize that though the abuse inflicted on me had stopped, its effects still had me in its clutches. I had spent my adult life trying to escape the feelings by medicating them and instead continued to experience a lack of safety and a lack of control over my life. It all made sense. That's why I struggled to tell my story and even to find my words.

Feeling Safe Enough to Open Up

It was a little after four weeks of being in rehab, having gone from primary to extended care, when I experienced an incident. Our regular group counselor was out for the day, so another counselor filled in for him. I walked into the room to sit down next to the other six men and noticed the counselor. He was a bit older and shorter than me, bald, and dressed casually. After my group exchanged greetings with one another, we quieted down and waited for the session to start.

I noticed the counselor looking at me. I felt very uncomfortable. Then, in a very pointed manner and in the presence of all the other men, he said, "Tell us about the sexual abuse with your dad."

I froze.

Before I could even catch my breath, one of the younger guys in the group joked around and said, "Yeah, tell us the juicy details."

I thought I was going to die.

My breathing became shallow, my head was spinning, I had hot flashes, and I began to sweat. The panic was taking over my body. Though I had played the abuse over and over in my head a million times, I had never verbalized what happened, never in my life.

I sat there, stunned. Though I am not sure how I did it, I managed to choke out, "I'm not ready to talk about it." The counselor tried to encourage me to talk, but I couldn't; I didn't have the words. It was an intensely painful moment.

The young man's joke might have been the most

unnerving part for me. I understand that the guy might have felt uncomfortable in the group and with the question, so his lighthearted approach and thoughtless comment were his way of dealing with it. Indeed, in my own life, I often joked in other ways about my childhood experiences. Nevertheless, the whole incident shook me up.

One of the prominent themes in group sessions was telling our stories. Besides counseling, education, and other programs, telling our stories was a key component in our journey toward healing. I heard other people's stories and knew my narrative was far different and much more disturbing. I wasn't comfortable telling it.

I became really good friends with a Christian guy in rehab. (I'll refer to him as Brennan.) Brennan said to me, "If you're not ready to talk about it, don't. But make sure when you get out of here that you find someone you feel safe with so you can get your story out and find healing."

Brennan was a Godsend to me. One day, we were sitting in my room, and I shared a tiny bit of my childhood story. While he looked shocked, he was very understanding and compassionate.

I admired Brennan. He was just beginning his career in the medical field, and though he was not trained in counseling, his wisdom in permitting me not to share my story until I felt safe was a huge encouragement to me. The psychiatrist I first met in rehab gave the same message as Brennan did: take your time and share your story when you feel safe to do so. Brennan knew intuitively how much I was struggling with sharing my story, so he gave me those wise words: "If you're not ready to talk about it, don't talk about it." I felt safe in those words.

For several days following that group session, I felt hyper-aroused, keyed up, and very anxious. I wanted to disappear! At the same time, I knew that God was working and my healing journey had just begun. It was only four-and-a-half weeks earlier that I had cracked the door open on my secret of being sexually abused.

I would find in the coming weeks and months that this difficult moment at extended care was also a pivotal point in my healing journey. Finding healing and a sense of wholeness is a process, often one that progresses slowly, one step at a time. I would eventually find the words, speak the words, and embrace the words of my story, but I had a long way to go before that would take place.

HIDING IN PLAIN SIGHT

I've been asked if Debbie knew I was abused as a kid or if I hid it from her. The reality is that I hid it from myself. To some extent, I was consciously aware of parts of the abuse. I had thoughts about it and would sometimes even casually joke about certain things that happened in my childhood home. However, I didn't allow myself to experience emotions about it.

Trauma and abuse survivors often compartmentalize parts of their stories. We separate our feelings and emotions from the facts. That's why, during the intake process at rehab, I could factually state that I was sexually abused as a child and initially tell the psychiatrist peripheral information about it. But when it came to the group discussions and sharing my story, I never talked about my childhood incidents in any detail. I never shared my story from a place of emotion. I had compartmentalized those feelings into a locked room. I had buried them deep underground. I had repressed them.

There was an internal war taking place. The left brain, which is responsible for thoughts, was very active in my life. I had many, many thoughts regarding my abusive childhood. However, the right brain, which is focused on the emotional impact of my abuse, was shut down. Though sharing my story was a big part of my healing journey, which is why I was encouraged to do so in rehab, that part of my story was also something I had promised myself I would never talk about.

This message was conveyed to me when I was still a child, that these things I experienced should never be discussed. I internalized this rule in my early childhood and carried it through my mid-fifties. Dr. Claudia Black, in her book *It Will Never Happen to Me*, points out that families with chemical dependency have three rules: "You don't talk. You don't trust. You don't feel."[6] It's a good description of how I had coped, how I had survived.

Then I went to rehab, and for the first time in my life, I had to confront these thoughts—not in a factual or academic way, but from my heart and the depths of my soul. Though I battled sharing my story, I wanted to talk. I wanted to trust. I wanted to feel. But I had no clue how to do it.

DEFRAGGING MY NARRATIVE

People who have suffered trauma often have an incoherent narrative. It's difficult for us to place events correctly in life's timeline. In other words, I wasn't able to say that I was four when this happened, seven when this happened, and nine when this happened. My memories were all jumbled up and fragmented. For me to get a more coherent and linear grasp of my story, it needed to be defragmented, also known as defragging.

I like the definition of *defragging* that applies to computers because it's easy to see the parallels to the process of defragmenting my own story:[7]

> Defragmentation, also known as "defrag" or "defragging," is the process of reorganizing the data stored on the hard drive so that related pieces of data are put back together, all lined up in a continuous fashion.
>
> You could say that defragmentation is like cleaning house for your Servers or PCs, it picks up all of the pieces of data that are spread across your hard drive and puts them back together again, nice and neat and clean.
>
> Defragmentation increases computer performance.

This definition clearly shows the need for taking all the scattered pieces of data—memories, flashbacks, emotions, bodily sensations, responses, etc.—spread across your hard drive (your left and right brain, your heart, your soul) and putting them back together in a more continuous fashion. Defragging your story begins to provide a more coherent narrative.

The thinking part of the brain goes offline and is somewhat unavailable when trauma occurs. That is why details are so hard to recall clearly. So often, people who go through trauma have parts of their lives they don't remember, or they don't remember when certain events took place.

Several years after rehab, as I was walking down my driveway one day, a memory of my childhood popped up, and I thought, *"Oh wow, that happened."* It's a sign of healing when the memories no longer feel so horrific that I can't allow them to become part of me and my story.

Defragging my narrative has been stressful and painful because memories are coming into my mind and I'm having flashbacks that take me out of the present and bring me into the past, but it's also a real sign of healing. It's yet another sign that God is walking with me on this long but hopeful path.

THE SOURCE OF MY ENCOURAGEMENT

Trauma affects every area of our lives. Because I am a Christian, it also affected my relationship with God, at least how I believed God felt about me. This came from the guilt and shame I experienced, which told me I was deeply marred and unable to be loved.

I read a quote from Pastor Tyler Minton that mirrored how I often felt. He said, "I lived convinced that at best God tolerated me and at worst He hated me, that I had ruined His plan for my life, and even if I somehow got my act together, it would never be as good as what He originally planned."[8]

Though I struggled with these feelings and thoughts, I also knew Jesus had shown up in my mess and was walking with me on this journey. Throughout this lengthy process of rehab and beyond, I started to experience my faith in a new way.

While I was in extended care, Debbie sent me a card with Bible verses on it to encourage me. Even though I had read the verses before, studied them at Bible College, and preached them, there was something different when I read them in rehab. They became alive to me in a prominent and authentic way.

Hebrews 4:12 says, "For the word of God is alive and active." First Peter 1:23 says, "For you have been born again, not of perishable seed, but of imperishable, through the living and enduring word of God." One verse especially spoke to my heart, so much so that I clung to it time and again: "'For I know the plans I have for you,' declares the LORD, 'plans to prosper you and not to harm you, plans to give you hope and a future'" (Jeremiah 29:11).

All the Scriptures Debbie sent me popped off the page. They encouraged me and gave me tremendous hope. I would go outside on the grounds of the rehab campus, sit on an Adirondack chair, and read the verses repeatedly. I would end my long days by lying in bed and holding the card on my chest, reading the verses over and over again.

GOING HOME: THE END OF REHAB AND THE START OF RECOVERY

The night before I was scheduled to leave rehab, I asked if I could treat the other guys in extended care to a pizza party. It was approved by the staff, and everyone attended the celebration. Before the party, at the last group session, everyone talked about the impact of having me as a part of his journey. It was very emotional, but left a good feeling. There was also pain associated with it, as I had spent the last two months with them and gotten to know them. I wondered if I would ever see any of them again.

The next morning, I packed my things into my bag. Before walking out of my room, I took the card with Bible verses Debbie had sent me. Sitting on my bed, I read Jeremiah 29:11 aloud: "'For I know the plans I have for you,' declares the LORD, 'plans to prosper you and not to harm you, plans to give you hope and a future.'"

That day, my last day in extended care, Debbie and I had a session with my counselor. We talked about what would happen as I moved forward in my healing. Debbie set limits and boundaries and shared her expectations regarding my behavior when I returned home. We also discussed my next phase of treatment, which would officially launch me into recovery.

It was agreed that I would go to intensive outpatient therapy several times a week. (Intensive outpatient therapy is sometimes referred to as an intensive outpatient program, or

IOP for short.) Besides intensive outpatient therapy, I would also go to a counselor for quite some time. Finally, I would go to Narcotics Anonymous (NA). The suggestion was that I go to ninety meetings in ninety days. That was a challenge for me. I didn't want to run into clients, so I knew I had to go out of my local area to maintain anonymity.

I thought about the future. On one hand, I was looking forward to being home with my wife. On the other hand, I was very tense about leaving this place. Rehab had come to represent safety. My days and nights were predictable and carefully scheduled. I was surrounded by other people who were facing their battles and on a journey to find healing within their stories, just as I was. I suddenly felt a sense of real emptiness. I looked at my wife and my counselor, and I thought to myself, *"Now what, Lord?"*

Chapter Three Reflections

Question: Are aspects of your past unclear? Do they need defragging? How does the thought of approaching that process make you feel? What steps would you need to take to begin this process?

___

___

___

___

___

___

___

___

___

Question: Is there someone in your life with whom you feel safe? Have you shared your story with this person? If not, what is stopping you?

Question: Do you know any Bible verses you can cling to for hope on your healing journey?

Chapter Three Notes

Part B: Childhood

CHAPTER FOUR

I Was Taught That Life Is Unsafe

Childhood should be carefree, playing in the sun; not living a nightmare in the darkness of the soul.[9]

—Dave Pelzer

Graphic Content Warning: *Some of the content in this chapter shares graphic descriptions of child abuse. It has the propensity to trigger people who have struggled with child abuse, trauma, or addiction. If this describes you, the reader, I encourage you to put the book down and find someone experienced in child abuse, trauma, or addiction recovery to read this book with you, rather than reading it alone. If you have been abused or are being abused, please reach out to an abuse hotline. If you're in the U. S., please contact the National Sexual Assault Hotline by calling 800.656.HOPE (4673) or via online chat at https://hotline.rainn.org/online. They will assist you on your path to freedom.*

EVEN THE HOUSE HAS A HISTORY

Before I was born, chaos prevailed in what would be our home. The house I grew up in had an eerie history before my parents even moved into it. The original owners had built the ranch-style house themselves. It was an early version of a custom home. Though the house was nice, what went on in it was far from pleasant. The couple, as I've been told, were plagued by domestic violence. I can remember a closet door in our living room. When you opened it, you could see a bullet hole that was sloppily patched.

One day, the couple got into a huge fight, and the wife called the state police for help. When the trooper arrived at the home, he tried to mediate the fight, but to no avail. The husband, who was in a rage on his front porch, which would eventually become our front porch, ended up being shot and killed by the trooper.

Considering the violence I witnessed and experienced in my childhood, I look back at this incident and see it as prophetic. Interestingly, my mother told me this story repeatedly throughout my childhood. It would become one of many traumatic stories and experiences I was exposed to as a child.

Another story I often heard was when I had pneumonia at the early age of two-and-a-half years old. It was so severe that I ended up in the hospital in an oxygen tent. During my hospital stay, which was in December, my mom told me that my grandmother (her mom) was also in the hospital, dying from cancer. On top of that, my mom's brother died of a heart attack at the age of thirty-one. All of this occurred while I was in the hospital with pneumonia. In subsequent years, my mom would often say, "I hold my breath getting through the holidays."

My life seemed to be plagued with trauma right from the very beginning, but sadly the trauma would intensify into a disastrous story.

My Father—Hurt, Humiliation, and Pain

It was time for dinner, and I was really hungry. As soon as my mom put the plates down in front of us, I knew I didn't want to eat the orange vegetable, cooked carrots. I gobbled up the other food on my plate.

Suddenly, my father, noticing I wasn't eating the carrots, screamed out, "Eat the damn carrots now!"

I didn't want to eat them, but I was scared of what he might do to me. I started shaking but knew not to cry. Crying just made things worse.

Irate, he reached over and began forcing the carrots into my mouth. I froze, unable to speak because I started gagging on the carrots. I couldn't chew and swallow them as fast as my father was shoving them into my mouth. He didn't stop. I felt sick and was having a tough time breathing. All of a sudden, I vomited all over the dinner table.

Without warning, my dad, now even more enraged, picked me up and threw me into the trash. "Stay there," he said. "That's where you belong. You're a piece of garbage!"

I was only four years old when my dad forced carrots down my throat, which could have choked me to death, then threw me into the garbage.

The dining table was rectangular and seemed big. It fit my parents, me, and my two siblings. There was a light hanging from the ceiling over the table.

We always sat in the same places. My mom would sit at one end of the table, and my dad would sit at the other. I sat next to my dad, my sister sat next to me, and my brother sat across from us.

I have no memory of how everyone else at the table reacted to what my dad did to me. I'm also not sure how long I was in the garbage or who removed me from it.

A strange thing happened when I was twenty-eight years old. My wife, Debbie, and I went to a wedding in upstate New York. It was a beautiful and elaborate affair. We were having a fun time and looking forward to the delicious meal. We were served our plates, and I was thrilled to see steak and potatoes, a couple of favorite foods of mine. There were also cooked carrots. I honestly didn't give it a second thought. The carrots looked appetizing, so I took a bite of one. I immediately began to gag. It was like I was transported back to being four years old, and my body was once again responding to the trauma I had experienced at that dinner table.

To this day, I cannot eat cooked carrots.

"Mark, come to the kitchen."

I heard my father call out to me, but I didn't want to go. Even though I was young, I knew if I didn't go to him, it would only make things worse. I knew not to cry as I walked toward the kitchen. Whenever I cried, he would become furious.

"Mark!"

I walked into the kitchen and saw my dad sitting in a chair.

"There you are. Come stand in front of me."

I walked over and stood right in front of him.

He didn't look me in the eyes; he just stared at my pants. "Now stand still, Mark." He pulled down my pants and my underwear so that they were at my feet. He started inspecting my private parts, my penis.

I didn't look down at what he was doing. I tried to look at anything but him. As I felt the pain, I froze. It was such horrible pain and humiliation, yet I didn't say a word! Trying desperately not to react with the fear that was in my heart, I looked down and saw my father obsessively inspecting my penis. He stuck a sewing needle in different parts of it. I don't remember what happened next, but I recall I vowed never to tell another soul what had happened to me.

One of the first memories that came flooding back to me in rehab was this incident in the kitchen with my dad inspecting my penis. Again, I was only four years old when that happened, and it would continue to happen in the kitchen for years.

It became obvious to me that my addiction to prescription medications kept both my memories and the anxiety of the trauma I experienced at bay. As soon as I was off the meds, memories came flooding back into my mind. This memory that took place in the kitchen came back with a vengeance.

The house was unusually quiet. My mom had gone to bed early. I curled up on the couch in the living room as my dad watched the news. After a little while, my father invited me to lie on the recliner with him. I held my breath, but he didn't seem irritated or annoyed, so I relaxed a bit.

Though apprehensive, I was glad my dad was not angry. I took him up on the invitation to join him in his chair. As I lay on his chest, he continued watching TV, but soon I could feel his hand move down my back, inside my pajamas and underwear. I held my breath, not sure what would happen next. Was he going to use the needle again? Instead of inspecting my private parts, he started rubbing them with his hand.

Before long, he was doing things I didn't understand. I didn't know how to feel. Feelings of dread, excitement, and confusion surged through my body. He kept watching the news, and I was trying not to react, hoping it would all stop very soon. While I hated it, honestly, I loved the attention from and connection with my father.

I have clear memories of my dad caressing and fondling my body, amongst other things, in the living room. That wasn't the only place it happened. It also took place in the kitchen, the bathroom, and my parents' bedroom—from when I was four until I was around seven years old.

My dad was a very driven and determined man, and the sexual abuse he inflicted on me in my childhood was no exception. As a consequence, I was a child who walked around in a constant fog. Besides often being confused, I had tremendous difficulties with focusing and paying attention. Though I didn't know it at the time, I was dealing with the trauma and abuse I suffered in my childhood through depersonalization, derealization, and disassociation.

MY UNPREDICTABLE AND DANGEROUS CHILDHOOD

Our house was the only one on the street, and across from our house was a truck garage with a refueling station that had both gas and diesel. My dad, who owned a construction company, also owned the garage and fueling station.

When I was about five or six years old, my dad decided to burn the garage down so he could collect the insurance money. Hundreds of gallons of gas were *right next* to the garage my dad was going to torch. What could possibly go wrong with a dangerous, fraudulent scheme like that, right?

He lit the garage on fire, but the flames got out of control and started crawling toward the underground gas tanks as well as the above-ground fuel pumps. My dad came running into the house, screaming, "Get under the beds. It's going to blow!"

Imagine being a little kid and being told the place was

going to blow up. My nervous system was constantly overactivated. I was always feeling anxious and on guard, waiting for the next dangerous or traumatizing event to happen.

A child's brain needs a predictable environment to develop, but I faced continual unpredictability, chaos, and trauma. If you go to the doctor and hear a bad report, your body responds to the emotions you are feeling. When you get into a car accident, you become anxious, and your body responds to that physically. Our bodies were not created to be in a continuous state of upheaval, yet in my childhood, that's exactly what I experienced: a constant state of fear, anxiety, anger, and chaos. My brain needed consistency, but I never got it. My emotional and personal development needed stability, but I never felt safe.

I lived in a kind of daze throughout my childhood. I couldn't focus or concentrate well. I certainly didn't feel secure at home or at school. While some children will feel safe in one place or another, I carried my insecurities with me wherever I went. I felt lost, both physically and emotionally. I struggled a lot with schoolwork because the stress I carried caused me to be easily distracted.

The one thing I learned quickly in childhood, the thing I embedded into my heart, was that life was scary and unsafe. As Bessel van der Kolk, MD, points out in his book *The Body Keeps the Score: Brain, Mind, and Body in the Healing of Trauma*, "After trauma, the world is experienced with a different nervous system that has an altered perception of risk and safety."[10]

I didn't feel safe anywhere because safety is found within oneself. When you don't feel safe in your own body, it doesn't matter what environment you are in; you just don't feel safe.

In her book *Allies in Healing: When the Person You Love Was Sexually Abused as a Child*, Laura Davis wrote, "Abuse manipulates and twists a child's natural sense of trust and love. Their innocent feelings are belittled or mocked, and they learn to ignore their feelings. They can't afford to feel the full range of feelings in their body while they are being abused—pain, outrage, hate, vengeance, confusion, arousal. So, they short-circuit them and go numb. For many children, any expression of feelings, even a single tear, is cause for more severe abuse. Again, the only recourse is to shut down. Feelings go underground."[11]

Other Levels of Sadness

I finally started going through the journey of processing my childhood when I entered rehab and followed that up with individual counseling as well as an intensive out-patient program (IOP). Part of the process was allowing my emotions to come to the surface. That was no small task since there were so many layers of feelings that needed to be addressed, feelings I had spent a lifetime repressing. As Dr. Claudia Black aptly stated, the family rules in the home of abuse are: Don't talk; don't feel; don't trust.[12] I followed those rules my whole life until I finally started facing my addictions, which eventually broke the seal on the secrets of my childhood. It has been an exceedingly arduous process. On one hand, I was conditioned not to go against the family rules. On the other hand, if I didn't go against the family rules, I would never experience healing.

When I started to confront my memories and feelings of childhood, it was like a disheveled and chaotic flurry of emotions. I could feel anger, confusion, sadness, fear, and brokenness all at the same time.

One of the saddest aspects I've had to deal with regarding my abusive and traumatic childhood was the following type of provocative question:

> *Where was my mom in all of this?*
>
> *Where was she when I was force-fed to the point of gagging?*
>
> *Where was she when I was thrown into the trash and told I was garbage?*
>
> *Where was she when I was having needles stuck into my penis?*
>
> *Where was she when I was being sexually abused all over the house, repeatedly, for years?*
>
> *Where was she when the building across the road burned down?*
>
> *Where was she?*

I didn't know the answers to those questions then, and I still don't have the answers today. Honestly, I'll probably never know. What I do know is that those unanswered questions add layers of sadness to my story.

Back then, however, at the ripe age of seven or eight years old, there was something I did know. I knew I had a dream to become a therapist so I could help others. Later in life, I earned my degrees for that job.

Chapter Four Reflections

Question: Did your parents or anyone else ever force you to do something that felt uncomfortable or unsafe?

____

____

____

____

____

____

____

____

____

____

Question: What was the atmosphere in your home when you were growing up? In what ways does that impact how you approach life today?

Question: What are some unanswered questions that have added sadness to your story? Is there anyone with whom you could explore those questions? How might God bring you comfort in the face of unanswered questions?

Chapter Four Notes

CHAPTER FIVE

When Things Aren't As They Appear

There are wounds that never show on the body that are deeper and more hurtful than anything that bleeds.[13]

—Laurell K. Hamilton

Even though I was young, I knew my dad was an important man in our community. He owned a construction company, and he was the Chairman of the Board of a local bank. People admired and respected him. It was quite different from how he and my mom grew up. They both came from humble beginnings, growing up extremely poor during the Depression era. Although my dad didn't even graduate from high school because of a motorcycle accident during his senior year, he was driven to become successful. In fact, he was so successful that he became a multimillionaire. Yet, how my dad appeared to the outside world was vastly different from how my siblings and I experienced him.

Everything looked good on the outside. My dad was praised and held up as a pillar in the community, but at home, he was the man who did unseemly things to me, the man I wanted to hide from as soon as I heard him come home. As a young child, I never understood how people could commend and glorify the man who abused me, and that only added to my confusion.

My dad's sexual abuse started when I was four and continued until I was seven years old. It stopped when our family experienced our first robbery. That's not a typo. There were two robberies in the McNear house: one actual robbery, which I'll explore now, and one thwarted robbery, which I'll explore later in the chapter.

The Armed Robbery

When I was seven years old, my family experienced the devastation of an armed robbery in our home. My siblings and I were asleep through the whole experience. After it happened, we heard the details of what occurred from our mom and dad. Over the years, our parents regularly talked about it. The topic consumed our home.

It took place on the evening of June 1. My aunt and uncle were over for dinner. A bit earlier in the evening, my father received a call from a man saying he and his co-workers needed to meet with him about a construction job. My dad, knowing my aunt and uncle would be visiting, told them they needed to meet on another night. The caller pushed back, so my father agreed to meet.

Initially, two men came to the side door, and my dad let them in. Almost immediately, they brandished guns and then asked my dad to switch on the outside lights (which we later came to understand was a signal to notify the other two men). After that, the two other men, also armed, came into the house.

Two men went upstairs where my siblings and I were sleeping. We never woke up during all of this, but we were told they were watching us, guns ready, to see if we would stir. The other two men, who stayed downstairs, tied up the adults and spent an hour packing and hauling money out of the house. Strangely, the men seemed to know where to look for the valuables that were hidden in various places upstairs. They took about $100,000 in diamonds and cash, my dad's rare coin collection that was stashed in a vault in the basement, as well as our personal paperwork.

The four robbers were apprehended, and it was found that they were already serving time for crimes they committed before the robbery. That caused even more stress in our home as we were inundated with police visits and court appearances. Our home life was always chaotic, but our world turned upside down after the robbery.

THE AFTERMATH: CHAOS AND DYSFUNCTION CONTINUED TO SPIRAL OUT OF CONTROL

Can an already completely chaotic home get even more chaotic? Unfortunately, in my household, the answer to that question was yes. The robbery had a huge effect on the entire family. Even though I slept through it, the constant talk about it, combined with the abysmal dysfunction that came from it, gave me repetitive nightmares. Crying myself to sleep became a nightly occurrence.

My mom seemed scared all the time, and my dad became paranoid. Shotguns were leaning against the walls in the corners of the living room and my parents' bedroom. There were shotgun shells on a shelf nearby, along with cans of mace.

We were kept home from school for the rest of the school year because my parents were afraid we would be kidnapped. Since my dad was Chairman of the Board of a local bank and the robbers had taken all of our personal records, including Social Security cards, he and my mom were concerned someone would try to kidnap us for ransom, knowing the bank would pay it. Imagine the fear my siblings and I had about being kidnapped. While we watched TV or ate our meals, I regularly heard my parents chat about all of it in the background. Most of what happened was outside of my understanding at the time, but there was one thing I did understand: the dangerous prospect of going back to school.

Though the robbery affected all of us, it changed my mother drastically, perhaps more than the rest of us. Her anxiety took over. She battled post-traumatic stress disorder (PTSD) and often complained about being dizzy or having a "floaty head." Mom appeared preoccupied and had difficulty paying attention. She seemed overwhelmed with everything. Though we would eat meals at the dinner table off and on, it became more off than on.

Besides the PTSD, my mother also became an alcoholic. I remember her sitting at the kitchen table, smoking cigarettes and becoming intoxicated. As an eight-year-old child, I was devastated to see my mother in this condition—so much so that when she would step out of the room, I would dump some of the beer out of her bottles and add water to them. It was not only my way of slowing down the intoxication process, but also my attempt to gain some control over a family that was completely unraveling.

Though he rarely said anything verbally, my dad would get incredibly frustrated, rolling his eyes and sighing, when my mom was intoxicated. There were many nights when she went to bed around six or seven o'clock in the evening, always saying, "I've had enough of this day." It was heartbreaking to see my mom self-destruct before my eyes.

MY DAD'S PARANOIA

The aftermath of the armed robbery affected my dad as well. Though he always had a propensity for paranoia, the robbery accelerated it exponentially. He decided we needed to have a secret place to hide money, rare coins, and other valuables.

In our basement, there was a cement wall, which he broke through. Then he gave my sister and me utensils—forks, knives, and spoons—to dig out dirt from the hole in the cement wall. Dad also made sure we had a bucket to put the dirt in.

Interestingly, I remember my dad warning me never to tell anyone about it. However, a family friend came up to me in 2021 and asked, "Do you remember that room your father had down in the basement with all of the coins and silver bars and money?" He went on to give me details, stating my dad brought him in to show him the room. I was stunned!

Creating a secret hiding spot in the basement was one of many ironies when it came to my dad. Out of fear of being robbed, he wanted a safe room, and he wanted to keep it a secret. Then he told someone about that room, even brought him into it, after telling me not to say a word.

Another irony is that he owned a construction company. I understand why he didn't use his professional crew to do the job, but why didn't he at least borrow some of the tools? Instead, he had his youngest children dig out a space with forks, knives, and spoons, which is absolutely bizarre.

Lastly, my dad was the Chairman of the Board at the local bank. Why didn't he keep his rare coins and valuables in safe-deposit boxes at the bank, instead of storing them at home, especially after experiencing an armed robbery? It's strange, right?

Shortly after the robbery, we found out that it was set up by my uncle, who was visiting us the day the armed men invaded our home.

When Outside Terror Struck a Second Time

It was a warm spring day when I came home from school. I was feeling cranky and irritable, not surprising for a ten-year-old boy.

My mom called out, "Mark, empty the vacuum cleaner!"

"Oh man, not that." I hated doing that chore. I needed to take the vacuum outside, walk across our dead-end street into a field, and clean it. I called back begrudgingly, "Okay, mom," and consented to my mom's request. My mom would obsessively ask me to do things over and over when they did not get done right away, and that drove me crazy. I took the vacuum across the street to empty it, and when I walked back into the house, I mumbled, "It's done." I put the vacuum away in the closet next to the front door.

Just after I had entered the house and put the vacuum away, there was a knock on the door. My mom nervously got up from the couch and bolted toward the door. Before she had a chance to check that the door was locked, a man on the other side pushed it open, uninvited.

"Oh no!" I thought. I had left the door ajar and unlocked! This was absolutely taboo. The front door (and all other doors in our house) needed to be secured immediately upon entering. Of course, the cause for this was the horrible armed robbery we had experienced just three years before.

Mom greeted the man near the door, who began mumbling and tripping over his words. He said something about his car breaking down on Route 80 and that he needed to call his insurance company to get help. As this was happening, my sister loaded a shotgun in the corner of the room and pointed it toward the front door.

As the man continued to fidget and ramble on, my mom noticed a second man coming up the outside stairs. My mom promptly slammed the door closed and locked it. The men disappeared quickly after their failed attempt to break in.

While all of this was happening, I managed to make my way to the closet without being noticed. Inside the living room closet, there were two buttons. One button activated the alarm when we were leaving the house. The other button, which I referred to as "the panic button," triggered a loud noise outside our home while also notifying the local police department. Panicked, I kept hitting the alarm button, but the alarm wasn't going off. Later, I realized I was hitting the activation button, not the panic button. Eventually, my sister hit the panic button.

The police arrived promptly, two cars and two officers. I watched as they stood in the living room, asking questions about the ordeal. I could see that the police officers looked concerned and serious. One of the officers carefully took notes as my mom gave them the facts about the incident. My sister and I added various details we believed to be important.

Shortly after the police arrived, my dad came home. Mom explained what had happened while my sister and I stood there, watching the conversation. Somewhere in the recounting of the story, my mom mentioned that I had left the door unlocked and ajar after cleaning the vacuum.

My dad, who until that moment had been focused on my mom and the police, turned and looked at me with a glare I interpreted as utter disgust. I could feel myself shaking as I wondered what might happen after the police officers left. Oddly, my dad never talked about it with me again, but the look he gave me spoke volumes.

Later that evening, I felt exhausted. I went to the bathroom to take a bath. I glanced out the bathroom window before turning the water on, and I could see the headlights of cars traveling on Route 80. Suddenly, my body began to shake, and I experienced shortness of breath. I held on to the bathroom sink. I was dizzy, my face was hot, and my body felt weak. I didn't know what was happening. (Years later, I realized I was experiencing my first panic attack.)

I didn't leave the bathroom to tell anyone in my family what I was experiencing. Deep down, I believed I had caused the day's events to occur. I was the one who had left the door ajar and unlocked. I thought, *"I deserve to feel the way I do."*

My Dad's Abuse Continued to Haunt Me

When I was twelve years old, I suffered the worst stomach pain I had ever experienced. I remember lying on the couch in the living room, crying and in agony. I called out for help from my mom and dad, but my dad became extremely angry. He started screaming and swearing at me for eating too many M&Ms.

At that point, there were two pieces of information I wanted to share with my dad. One, we didn't have any

M&Ms in the house. And two, I hadn't eaten any candy whatsoever during the entire day! However, I knew my dad was not the most rational of men, so I kept my mouth shut.

As the pain increased, my dad finally realized something was genuinely wrong with me. He decided to drive me, along with my mom, to the hospital. I'm amazed we even made it to the hospital, considering how recklessly my dad was driving. If you have ever been to Disneyland, I would compare my trip to the hospital to Mr. Toad's Wild Ride. When we got to the hospital, they confirmed in the exam room that I had appendicitis and needed surgery.

Then something happened that I will never forget. To prepare me for surgery, they needed to shave my pubic hair. I was petrified. My anxiety heightened as a nurse, who happened to be male, touched me around the genital area, and all the memories and thoughts of the sexual abuse I endured as a child at the hands of my father came flooding back. The fear and discomfort I experienced related to my stomach pain, the need for surgery, and the surgery itself all paled in comparison to the fear and discomfort I experienced as the nurse was prepping me.

I recently went for hernia surgery, and those same thoughts and feelings bombarded me as I was examined and prepared for surgery. Again, the past is not the past when it shows up in the present.

A quote from Dr. Diane Langberg resonates with me and others who were abused as children. She wrote, "Contrary to popular belief, children are not resilient, a word which simply means they can return to their original state. They do not 'bounce back' from abuse."[14]

THE CAR CRASH THAT NEARLY ENDED MY LIFE

Teenagers crave autonomy and freedom, and I was no different. Having my own car was a means of escaping my tumultuous home life, even if only for temporary segments of time during the day or evening.

On New Year's Eve, at the age of nineteen, I was excited about meeting up with friends to celebrate. We had a long, enjoyable evening that took us into the wee hours of the morning. After the party, a group of us decided to go to a local diner for breakfast.

It was raining lightly when I headed back to my house. Suddenly, in what seemed like a split second, I saw a car swerve into my lane and come straight at me. I slammed on the brakes, but the car hit me head-on. My head hit the windshield. During the incident, I kept thinking, *"I'm going to have to remember all the details of this and explain it to my dad."* I think I was more afraid of my dad's rage about what happened than the seriousness of my injuries. I would later find out that the guy who hit me was drunk, three times over the legal limit of intoxication.

In the emergency room of the hospital, besides my many injuries, which included a broken femur, I was also diagnosed with a pulmonary embolism. My parents had been notified, and soon my father showed up in the emergency room, screaming at me. He yelled so much that the doctor had to have him removed from the area.

I was in the hospital for a month. I didn't know until I was on the mend that I was remarkably close to death in that emergency room. While I was there, I was given strong injections of painkillers. It soothed the physical pain, and it also reduced the anxiety I carried in my body, like the medications I would later misuse before going to rehab.

I thought about it then but did not fully realize as I do now that my world was upside down compared to what most families experience. There I was, lying in the emergency room, near death, less than an hour after being hit head-on by a drunk driver, and instead of my dad loving me, he shouted at me in such a rage that security had to take him away. To top it off, my mom developed agoraphobia after the accident and did not leave the house for weeks, months, sometimes up to a year at a time.

You Can Tear Down the House, But Where Do the Memories Go?

My childhood can be equated to a barrel filled with dysfunction, abuse, and rage. Any love was overshadowed by the turmoil. The terror that filled my heart was both physical and emotional. For some reason, I was often singled out as the object of my father's wrath. There were times, however, when all of us kids were blamed for my dad's unruly behavior.

One such time was when my mother and father were having a huge fight. My sister, my brother, and I were in the living room, watching TV, while the fight was taking place in front of us. My dad became so enraged that he grabbed a golf club out of his bag, which was sitting in the living room, and smashed the furniture, the TV, the knickknacks, and anything else he could find in the room. We just sat there, petrified.

He dropped the golf club on the floor, then turned to look squarely at us kids and said, "Look what you just made me do!" I recall him sitting on the floor, gluing things back together after the ordeal. What couldn't be fixed he replaced from a nearby furniture store. The room might have been restored, but my brain and body said otherwise.

Besides the painful experiences of my childhood, there were also oddities. I remember clearly when my dad would stand at the kitchen sink and wash piles of $100 bills. It was quite a process. He would use detergent and wash them gingerly in the water, making sure not to tear them or otherwise damage them in any way. Then he would dry them meticulously by pressing each bill tenderly between towels. It took quite a bit of time for the bills to dry. The last step to his cleaning process was to iron them. Yes, my dad washed and ironed $100 bills!

When they were all neatly clean and crisp, he would staple them in packs of $1,000, then put them in a metal box and place them in a secret, custom-made compartment in the living-room furniture. The bills in the box totaled $100,000.

Another bizarre part of my dad washing those bills is that,

for some reason known only to him, he didn't hide the money in the secret hiding place my sister and I had helped him to build in the basement. Instead, he hid it in the furniture. If I were to write down all of the oddities of my childhood, I'd probably have enough content to fill an entire bookcase!

The house I grew up in was torn down recently. A friend asked me how that made me feel, and my answer was as complicated as my childhood. I certainly felt relief. In a way, perhaps symbolically, it made me feel that the worst part of my life was indeed gone. I also felt sadness. It took so long for me to confront the abuse and the horror of my childhood, and I was finally in a place of recovery. I felt that the house being torn down meant I could no longer prove any of the things that went on there.

Chapter Five Reflections

Question: When have you felt unsafe? How has that affected your thoughts, emotions, and behaviors? Thinking about it now, what do you notice about how your body reacts?

Question: Have you ever blamed yourself for something that you truly did not have control over? If yes, what thoughts and feelings do you have regarding it?

Question: Have other people placed blame on you for things you weren't responsible for? How do you think that impacts your inner monologue toward yourself?

Chapter Five Notes

CHAPTER SIX

The Chaos That Shaped My Childhood

For God is not the author of confusion but of peace, as in all the churches of the saints.

—1 Corinthians 14:33 ***(NKJV)***

"This is all crazy," I thought as I stared up at the ceiling in my room. I wanted just one day without chaos, but that was too much to ask. I listened to my favorite music to find some peace. I knew there would soon be another drama, another fight, or another opportunity to suffer abuse.

As a teen, I knew my family life was strange. My childhood up to that point had been a series of traumatic experiences and outright mayhem. What I didn't realize at the time was that this way of life had become my norm, and I would carry that norm into my adulthood unless I transformed it.

THE LONG WALK HOME

My parents had a complicated relationship that could be volatile. When they fought, they really fought, and we all knew about it! My mom was often upset because of her suspicions that my dad was having an affair. She was right, which you will see later in this chapter. Considering my dad's temperament, oddities, and abusive ways, it isn't hard to understand why they had issues in their relationship. Of course, as with everything else in my childhood, my siblings and I were not spared from my parents' turmoil.

One evening when I was about ten years old, my family went to our local diner for dinner. As kids, we always enjoyed being able to eat out and get away from the awkwardness of the dinner table at home. While we were eating, my mom and dad got into a huge fight. He said something about her appearance, her hair. I remember being embarrassed and horrified that the drama of my family would play out in front of everyone at the restaurant.

My dad stormed out of the diner and drove somewhere, leaving us behind! My mom was terribly upset and decided that we needed to walk home, so my brother, my sister, and I walked out of the restaurant with our mom and started the long walk home. After the first mile or so, I remember complaining that my legs hurt. My mom, without looking at me and with determination in her voice, said, "Keep going. Just keep walking."

I'm not sure why I expected anything other than how she responded. She wasn't the type to show much affection, and she was often emotionally distant. Still, it wasn't the answer I was looking for. Considering we still had a few miles to walk, I was hoping for compassion, reassurance, or maybe a sit-down break. But like a soldier on a mission, my mom kept her eyes straight ahead and expected us to keep walking, no matter how far we had to go.

THE TEACHER WHO WAS A BULLY

As a child, I was always hoping for a place where I could feel safe. My home was anything but that. School had its challenges for me, as it does for many kids. There were the social dynamics of finding friends and trying to fit in or belong. As if that weren't enough, I also faced academic hurdles due to attention problems because of the trauma I endured at home.

When I was twelve years old and in sixth grade, I had a teacher whom my sister had a few years before me. My sister was a straight-A student and did very well in this teacher's class. This teacher might have expected me to be like my sister, but I was not. I was discombobulated and struggled with my schoolwork. I'm sure I disappointed my teacher, who singled me out as her target for humiliation.

This teacher was the epitome of a bully. She was very loud and critical, and I was always nervous around her. Even though she often mocked other students as well, I felt like I was the one who had the bullseye on my forehead. She never missed a chance to embarrass me, criticize me, and put me down in front of my peers.

I had real difficulties with organization, which meant my desk was always a mess. I lived in fear that she'd spot it one day, and eventually that day came. When my teacher saw my messy desk, she went on a rampage. She picked up the desk, dumped the contents out onto the floor—in front of the entire class, no less—and said to me, "You'll never go anywhere!"

I wished the classroom floor would open up and swallow me. I felt ashamed and humiliated. I simply wanted to disappear.

I went home, crying and distraught. My mom asked me what was wrong, and I told her every detail of what had taken place. Much to my surprise, my mom immediately acted and called the school. The following day, she met with the administration, and I was transferred to another class with a new teacher!

What really stood out to me, what I considered to be a big deal, was the fact that my mom had compassion on me and intervened with the school. I now know that's what parents are supposed to do, but in my family, it was not the norm.

Ironically, years later, I encountered my bully teacher as an adult. We were both teaching at the same college. I was teaching psychology, and she was an English professor. I ran into her on campus and reintroduced myself by saying, "Well, either I went somewhere, or you went nowhere." She just stared at me. There was no further discussion. It may seem a bit harsh that I said that, but it was my way of letting her know how deeply her words and behavior had impacted me.

The Power of Words

The tongue has the power of life and death, and those who love it will eat its fruit.

—Proverbs 18:21

My childhood was never easy, but when I was thirteen years old, I struggled with deep depression and intense anger. I was feeling very overwhelmed by my emotions and by my life in general. One day, I decided to confide in my dad that I wanted to take my own life. I will never forget his response. He looked at me and said, “If you’re that much of a fool, go ahead and do it.”

It wasn’t the feedback I was looking for. I’m not even sure what motivated me to tell him. I felt desperate and just blurted it out. I really shouldn’t have been shocked by what he said. My entire childhood consisted of verbal abuse from my father.

Chaos doesn’t allow for connection, and my mom and dad knew nothing but pandemonium. Disorder was their norm. Unfortunately for me and my siblings, we had no choice but to live with the effects of the chaos and parents who lacked interpersonal connection with their own kids. The combination of mayhem, alcohol abuse, mental health issues, and abusive behaviors made for one hellish childhood. For one reason or another, it seemed to me that out of the three of us kids, I received the lion’s share of verbal abuse.

When I was around eight years old, I got out of bed the

night before Easter. I walked into the living room and saw my parents bringing in Easter baskets, bunnies, and candy from the garage. My father saw me and became infuriated. He screamed, "Now look what you've done! You've wrecked Easter!"

It always seemed, by my dad's words, that I "wrecked things," I was "trash," I was "stupid," I was "inept," I was a "burden," and so much more. One comment I heard repeatedly out of my dad's mouth, especially when I became a teen, was: "What the hell's the matter with you? Are you a goddamn fool?"

I heard it when I shared my ideas or dreams for the future. I heard it whenever I took initiative to do something I had not done before. I heard it when I said I wanted to take flying lessons. I heard it when I wanted to wear a tuxedo for my eighth-grade graduation. I heard it whenever I had a different idea or opinion from my dad's. Not surprisingly, my dad's words took away my initiative in life and undermined my sense of personhood.

As incredibly bad as these words were, there was something my dad would say that was even more destructive to my character and feeling of self-worth. It revolved around my uncle, my father's brother. In those days, my uncle was called mentally retarded. Today, we would refer to his condition as mentally challenged, cognitively impaired, or intellectually disabled.

Repeatedly, through every stage of my childhood and into my teen years, my dad compared me to his brother and would often say, "You're just like my brother!" No matter what I did, even if it was homework (which my dad never sat down to help me with), I was compared to my uncle. My dad's message was clear.

The Bible says our words are powerful. What we say can bring life or death to someone. Our words have the power to bless or to curse someone. The message I received throughout my childhood was: "*There's something very wrong with me.*"

A Man Above the Law

My dad was a very influential person in our town. Everyone knew him, at least his outward persona. As both a successful businessman and Chairman of the Board of a local bank, my dad carried a lot of power in our community.

When I was about ten years old, my dad and I were driving on a back road in town. We heard a siren, looked in the mirror, and saw a police car with lights flashing, signaling us to pull over. I don't know if my dad was weaving as he drove, but I do know he was very annoyed at being pulled over.

The young police officer came to the window, and he recognized my father when he asked for his license and registration. My dad immediately started yelling at him, telling him that turning the lights on and blasting the siren was totally unnecessary. He laced his words with swearing to make sure the police officer heard him correctly. In the same breath, my dad told him to get back in his car and go down the road. Without batting an eye, that is exactly what the police officer did. I remember feeling bad for that young police officer.

My dad was used to getting whatever he wanted, and sometimes what he wanted was not in keeping with propriety. My mom and dad often fought about women, particularly the dalliances my mom believed her husband was having. I'm not sure how many affairs there were, but I do know there was one woman who was brought up often. It was the same woman my mom and dad fought about when he got angry and smashed everything in our living room with a golf club. Once, I even met this woman.

When I was about twelve years old, my dad took me to the house of a woman who was supposedly just his friend. I knew it was the same woman my parents had previously fought about, the woman my mom said my dad was too interested in. I remember feeling very uncomfortable about being in her house. Even as a kid, I sensed that my mom was not worried for nothing. As I watched them whisper and flirt with each other, my skin crawled. My dad seemed too familiar with the house, the setting, and the woman.

One day, my parents had another huge fight about this woman. He stormed out of the house, and my mom decided she couldn't take it anymore. I was in the living room and saw my mom take $20,000 in cash from a drawer in the office where $40,000 was stashed. She told me and my siblings she was going to the motel that was close to our house and directly instructed us not to mention a word about it to our dad. If he asked, we were expected to lie. She checked in under the alias Ruth Cole (her first name was Betty). I'm not completely sure what transpired, but she stayed at the motel for around fifteen days before returning home. My dad never knew she was there.

There was no doubt that both of my parents were abusive, each in a different way. My mom was neglectful and emotionally abusive in the way she manipulated and disconnected from her children. No kid should have to lie for a parent or pick one parent over another, but in my family, these things happened all the time.

Escape from Reality

Everyone has feelings of wanting to escape from reality at some point in life. For me, it was a daily desire. Even though I felt lonely, I would often isolate myself in my room to try to escape the madness of my home. Most often, I just wanted to disappear.

When I was around fourteen years old, my mom and dad went out for dinner, leaving me alone in the house. Normally, a teen would relish the opportunity to be home alone, but as much as I wanted a peaceful atmosphere, I was absolutely petrified to stay home alone since the armed robbery. In my desire to calm down and escape my anxiety, I decided to utilize my parents' whiskey cart by having a drink. It might have been a few drinks; I don't remember.

I had never had an alcoholic drink before, and after a short while, I became drunk. Of course, when my parents came home, I was nervous they would yell at me and worse. Oddly, they didn't even notice. When I went to my room, I kiddingly thought, *"Maybe it would be better around here if my dad drank."*

After that night, in fact, I would often kid around with my mom or my siblings that dad's mood and temperament might improve if he drank. Later, as an adult, I often joked about different horrible things that went on in my childhood. Though I didn't know it at the time, this was one of my ways of coping. To try to escape the trauma and abuse I endured during my years growing up, I would joke about the pain I experienced.

Looking back, I can see that I was always trying to find a way to escape the horrible reality of my young life. As a child and teen, I escaped by watching TV and listening to music endlessly. In my teen years, I also escaped into my fantasies of what I would become in the future, putting my hope in the prospect of doing something significant one day.

Little did I know that God had His hand on me and that through Him, not only would I experience much-needed transformation and healing in my life, but I would also have the privilege of helping other people to find freedom from their traumatic pasts.

Chapter Six Reflections

Question: Has anyone ever spoken something about you or compared you to someone in a way that impacted you deeply? Did those words impact you positively or negatively? How do you feel about those words now?

____

____

____

____

____

____

____

____

____

Question: Have you ever felt like you wanted to escape from the reality of life? What were you trying to avoid?

Question: Are there any unhealthy habits you have developed in an attempt to cope with difficult emotions and experiences? What are some alternative methods you might be able to utilize?

Chapter Six Notes

Part C: Recovery

CHAPTER SEVEN

Reconnecting with My Best Friend

> Healing comes when our story is raw, bone-deep, and full of hunger for what only Jesus can offer.[15]
>
> **—Dan B. Allender**

After rehab, a counselor with whom I had sessions spent time differentiating between *guilt* and *shame*. Guilt, I was told, is something I've done wrong or perceive I've done wrong. On the other hand, shame is an intrinsic feeling that I'm wrong, that there's something inherently wrong with me, or that I'm broken or flawed.

Shame is a deeply painful feeling. Because I felt terminally flawed, I felt unworthy of love and belonging. People who have been abused, especially as children, are not only ashamed of the acts of abuse, but often also have an intrinsic feeling that they are less than other people, that they are so deeply flawed that they cannot be loved. That's why so many abuse survivors believe they did something to cause their abuse. Instead of recognizing the abuser as being responsible for what he or she has done, the victim takes on the guilt, thinking, *"What did I do to cause this?"*

Was I Pursuing God, or Was God Pursuing Me?

After rehab, I felt lost and empty, yet I had hope. The most important thing I had done in rehab was to pursue my relationship with God. For too many years, I had moved away from my values and my faith, and that put my life further into a downward spiral. But when I came back to the Lord, I found His loving and accepting arms wide open for me.

Rehab was hard, and starting my prolonged period of recovery was just as difficult. A big part of recovery for me started with repentance. I was led to a particular scripture (Romans 2:4) that talks about God's kindness leading us to repentance. Instead of judging me, which was often how I felt, God was drawing me to Himself through "the riches of his kindness, forbearance and patience" (Romans 2:4). Entering my story with kindness rather than judgment has been integral to growth and healing.

A good friend of mine, Pastor Bruce Hoppe, has said to me countless times, "Don't let the dark places in your story overshadow the light of God's redeeming power." Throughout rehab, God was working in me, pointing out areas of my life that needed healing. I had to look at my struggles and my brokenness. I also had to look at the many unhealthy areas of my life, including my handling of and interactions with substances, food, lying, money, interpersonal relationships and codependency, intimacy, sex, and time management. All of these areas that needed healing had their roots in my childhood.

I wanted freedom and a new way to live. Romans 12:2 says, "Do not conform to the pattern of this world, but be transformed by the renewing of your mind. Then you will be able to test and approve what God's will is—his good, pleasing and perfect will."

When I returned home, facing the prospect of a long recovery, I continued pursuing my relationship with God. I found encouraging messages, books, podcasts, and YouTube videos. Everywhere I turned, there were messages on grace. Message after message focused on the prodigal son and accepting God's unconditional love for me despite my behaviors and brokenness. I found I could not get enough of God's Word. I read, listened to sermons, and went to church and Bible studies. I also prayed a lot more. Many times, I would write out prayers. I would also communicate with the Lord through my journaling.

God kept chipping away at my flawed perspective on how I thought He saw me, and He also showed me how I should view myself. Ephesians 2:10 was eye-opening for me! It says, "For we are God's masterpiece. He has created us anew in Christ Jesus, so we can do the good things he planned for us long ago" (NLT). The Lord continually brought this verse to my heart and mind.

Another verse that became vital to me in my recovery is 1 John 3:20: "Even if our hearts [feelings] condemn us, God is greater than our hearts [feelings], and He knows all things" (BSB). In my journey of healing, I have discovered an inner critic that often accuses me, berates me, and calls me names. Wow, I wonder where that came from.

It was important for me to understand that God restores people (Joel 2:12–32). No one is beyond His redemption and restoration. The closer I drew to the Lord, the more I saw His fingerprints on my life and in the details of my recovery.

One day, I read the following wonderful quote from Philip Yancey's book *Vanishing Grace*: "The Bible tells of flawed people—people just like me—who make shockingly bad choices and yet still find themselves pursued by God."[16] Things began to make sense. It wasn't that I was pursuing God; rather, it was the fact that God had been pursuing me.

LEARNING TO BE STILL

Though coming home from rehab was a tremendous change for me, my wife and I did work out a plan with the counselor regarding the path forward for my recovery. Debbie and I had agreed I would need to take time off from my practice to immerse myself fully in my recovery work. I was in no shape to counsel; I needed healing. So, while Debbie worked full-time, I focused on my NA (Narcotics Anonymous) meetings, my IOP (Intensive Outpatient Program), and my individual counseling sessions. I also spent a great deal of time growing in my faith through Bible study, books, audio messages, and church. Even though it may sound like a full plate, I had more time on my hands than what I had become used to in rehab.

Self-care was and is an important part of my recovery process, and it's something I had spent most of my life avoiding. It's interesting that as a licensed clinical social worker and psychotherapist, I had helped countless people with their problems and their pasts but had never thought about my own need for healing and recovery from trauma. There was a huge part of me that wasn't aware of how traumatized I was.

Learning the importance of self-care, such as going to doctor appointments and the dentist, seeing a nutritionist, and even spending time learning to play, has been an essential part of my healing. I found that taking time to play, or enjoy myself, was something I had to learn. That may sound strange, but my childhood did not include normal playtime or hanging out with friends. It had far more adult themes—dysfunctional adult themes at that—rather than the normal innocence of childhood laughter and play. I'm still working on this play thing!

One of the greatest challenges I had with starting my outpatient recovery was surrendering to the process of healing, because it felt counterintuitive. I had spent most of my life escaping my thoughts and feelings rather than dealing with them. To heal from my traumatic past, I had to face my thoughts and emotions while doing the opposite of what my feelings wanted me to do.

I remember telling Debbie in the beginning of my recovery that I just had to do everything opposite of what I felt. That was no easy task! In a way, it's true for everyone, because if we simply did whatever we felt like doing, we would be in trouble. However, it's especially true for people with addictions.

I wanted to do anything but experience my emotions. My mind was screaming at me to run away, to numb myself, to hide, to fight, or to medicate and shut down. The struggle caused a lot of noise in my head, like I had too many apps open on my phone or too many windows open on my laptop. At times, my anxiety was so high that I felt I could run a power plant for an entire city off the energy in my body. I was both physically and emotionally drained by the process.

I had to learn to regulate my emotions. A part of that process, as I learned, is that you can't have a relaxed mind unless your body is relaxed. Physical exercise, walks, playing with silly putty, using worry stones, doing mindfulness meditation, taking hot baths, journaling, and praying helped me to relax my body, which in turn helped to relax my mind. I have made progress, but I'm still climbing that mountain.

During this time, God gave me a scripture that guided me along this journey of quieting my mind, my body, and my reactions to my emotions. Psalm 46:10–11 says, "Be still, and know that I am God; I will be exalted among the nations, I will be exalted in the earth! The LORD of hosts is with us; the God of Jacob is our refuge" (NKJV).

Even amid the people's chaos and troubles (as recorded in Psalm 46), God called out to them to be still and know that He was God and He was with them. He was their refuge. This message pertains to all believers. When facing troubles, chaos, and problems, we can be still because of God. "Be still" means to cease striving, stop fighting, and stop relying on yourself and instead to rely on and trust God, believing He will fight the battle for you. Knowing God is with me and for me, I can be confident that He will see me through this process, which enables me to let go of my striving and relax in Him.

I knew my recovery journey would be a long, hard climb, but I also had the comfort of knowing I was not alone on this journey.

MY BRIDE, MY BEST FRIEND

When I returned home from rehab, I knew the first thing I wanted to do was reconnect with my wife. Debbie was and still is my best friend and soul mate, but my years of medicating my problems and trauma had inflicted a great deal of hurt on her. During rehab, she was able to write a letter that shared those hurts. As hard as it was to read, it was a catalyst in finding forgiveness and restoring our bond. When a friend of Debbie's asked her what it was like having me home from rehab, she said, "I feel like I got my husband back."

Debbie and I always had a great relationship, but our marriage suffered greatly as a result of my addictions. I needed to reconnect with her and build on the relationship we had. I think one of the things that helped us through this difficulty was that we had extensive counseling before we got married. We were both big believers in counseling, and we invested a lot of time walking through in-depth premarital counseling. The investment paid off in more ways than we ever expected it would. It made our reconnecting process that much easier.

When I got home from rehab, Debbie and I talked about so many things that had happened in my life and things I had done. Some of the things I shared with her were not easy for me to talk about, but her willingness to hear and to accept the things I was scared to talk about greatly strengthened the bond between us.

It was wonderful to start living life again as a couple. We started doing things with each other again, such as going out to dinner, shopping, talking about books we liked, going for walks, spending time with friends, going to movies, going pumpkin and apple picking, and more. There is a lot to be said for enjoying the normalcy of life together.

Debbie is a remarkable person. She truly is a woman of grace. Though she has talked about how I hurt her, she has never disparaged me or cut me down, though I'm sure I gave her good reason to do so. She never tried to change me but was supportive of me as I sought help and healing.

I can honestly say that Debbie showed me the love of God in how she handled my addictions, rehab, and the saga of my traumatic childhood. That inspired me to want to grow more and find the healing and transformation I very much needed.

Now, I'm not trying to paint a fairytale story. It's been hard on our marriage to go through all these things, but the deep connection I have with my wife is something I've never experienced before in my life. I am aware that many couples don't make it through the hardships and difficulties we have experienced. I'm blessed beyond measure that we are together and growing our marriage through my recovery process. Debbie is kind, insightful, wise, and godly. She really looks out for other people.

Our daughter has many of my wife's traits. Since Emily lived in Florida, our reconnection was by phone or texts, which takes longer than reconnecting in person. I had many amends to make with my daughter and made many apologies to her. I decided early on that I wouldn't tell her I was going to change. Instead, I would show her.

After getting out of rehab, I talked to Emily about it. She didn't know what to expect when I went back home. Would I stay clean? Would I remain sober? Or would I fall back into my old patterns? These were all reasonable questions on Emily's mind, and with her not living under our roof, it was harder for her to see my actions and daily routine.

In 2019, Emily married a wonderful man, Brandon, whom I love, respect, and admire. During the pandemic, they were in a place of transition and came to live with us for about a year. I remember thinking they would have the opportunity to see firsthand the progress I've made and the healing I've experienced. That was a time of restoration and connection for us, and we continue to grow in our relationship. I'm so grateful for their understanding and acceptance. I know this is not always the case in families. Emily, who now lives in Wyoming, is pursuing a degree to become a counselor, and I enjoy being able to send her different insights I have had during this healing journey.

I have found that a big part of my recovery and an integral part of healing has been reconnecting and renewing my relationships with God, my family, and others.

LEARNING TO ACCEPT MYSELF AND MY BROKENNESS

God clearly and gently guided me on my harrowing journey toward restoration and healing. I found a wonderful counselor by the name of Harry Flanagan. He works with Pure Desire Ministries, a Christian nonprofit organization that counsels those with addictions and sexual brokenness. One of the first things Harry said to me was: "We are going to go at your own pace. No pressure. No rushing the process."

Harry walked me through the pain of my sexual brokenness with acceptance, love, encouragement, and hope for my future. He often didn't comment or elaborate on what I said, but I knew and felt he cared deeply for me. Harry showed me kindness and love not only by the way he counseled me, but also in how he honored my story and held it as valuable.

As I worked with Harry, I wrote down the traumas I had experienced as a child. (Little did I know that, years later, I would write them down again for this book!) I found it interesting that the story I had so desperately tried to escape was presented as a path for my healing. I learned that I needed to embrace the stories and the pain to obtain freedom.

Harry recommended that I join a recovery group for men who struggle with addictions. When I was in rehab, I didn't want to be in a group, sharing my story. At first, I wasn't thrilled about the idea of doing it in recovery, either. But I trusted Harry and would learn how beneficial it is both to hear other's stories and to share my own. I also learned that God works in and through other people in our lives. Proverbs 27:17 says, "As iron sharpens iron, so one person sharpens another."

Eventually, I took Harry's advice and joined a recovery group. In time, I was able to tell my story. While the other men have stories different from mine, they accept me and help me to accept myself.

A good part of my recovery was found in fellowship with other men who had different stories but experienced similar problems. We learned to bear one another's burdens and to help each other out, and we are living proof that iron does sharpen iron. So much healing has taken place and will continue to take place in our men's recovery group. I believe each one of us is learning to build self-awareness, empathy for others, compassion, and a caring heart. To this day, years later, I still meet weekly with this group of men.

In his book *7 Pillars of Freedom Workbook*, Dr. Ted Roberts of Pure Desire Ministries wrote, "We get hurt in relationships, and the only place to get healed is in the context of relationships."[17] To that I say, "Amen."

There is no doubt I have found the Lord personified in other people. So many times on my path toward healing, the love of God has shown up in other people. Their kindness, love, understanding, grace, and acceptance come from the very heart of God.

My counselor, Harry, became a real father figure for me.

As you know, I didn't have the best father. But God used Harry in a profound way in my life. In fact, I know the Lord led me to Pure Desire Ministries and to Harry. It was no accident. God knew exactly what I needed, and in His love and kindness, He made sure I received it.

Restoration is a process, and it's not always a straightforward process, but God is in the business of redeeming and restoring people's lives. It's okay to travel the road toward recovery. Though it's a painful journey at times, it's also a truly satisfying one.

Chapter Seven Reflections

Question: When have you experienced shame or guilt? What is your understanding of the difference between shame and guilt? How has each impacted you?

Question: Are there areas of your life and healing journey that you have entered with judgment rather than kindness and compassion? How might you shift to approaching yourself with more compassion?

Question: Do you have an inner critic? Can you identify where it came from? In what ways can you combat and replace the voice of the inner critic with the truth of how God sees you?

___

___

___

___

___

___

___

___

___

___

___

___

Chapter Seven Notes

CHAPTER EIGHT

Feeling Alive!

God specializes in giving people a fresh start.[18]

—Rick Warren

Addictions cause your life to shrink. You withdraw from a normal routine, and you find it hard to be interested in or enjoy anything. Your life becomes very small.

But things changed for me during recovery. Now I wake up in the morning and look forward to the day. I enjoy doing things with Debbie. I look forward to seeing my clients. I look forward to going to church. I love talking to and spending time with friends. I can't wait to see my daughter and her husband when they come to visit.

You could say I have come alive! I've gone from a black-and-white life to one filled with vivid colors. I have even noticed that my ability to smell and taste things has improved tremendously.

It's not that I don't have any struggles or problems; I have plenty of those. I live daily with consequences that have come from the trauma I experienced. But God has truly given me a fresh start, and I love engaging in life.

RECOVERY IS A LIFELONG PROCESS

There are a lot of misconceptions about recovery for those who have suffered from trauma. Recovery is not a procedure, and it's not a linear process. It's not: do step one, then step two, then step three, and finally your trauma will be resolved and you will have recovered. No, recovery is not "one and done."

There's a tendency to want to make things better right away. You might say it's in our DNA. We all want instant healing, instant restoration, instant gratification, but the reality is that it can take years to see real progress and healing. Still, that shouldn't discourage anyone!

As Christians, we can see that God's process of transformation in our lives is not instant. Does the Lord ever change how we think, how we behave, or how we feel in an instant? Sure, He is God, and sometimes He heals or makes other changes in our lives suddenly. However, the process of transformation and sanctification in a believer takes place over an entire lifetime (Philippians 1:6). We will never be perfect in our human bodies, but we can experience God's transformation and restoration throughout our lives!

Individuals who have experienced trauma have been wounded. In fact, the Greek word for *trauma* is translated as "wound."[19] They have brokenness in their lives.

I've been in recovery for over seven years, and though I'm doing well, there are still issues I deal with daily. No matter who we are, as human beings, we will always have things to work on. First John 1:8 says, "If we say we have no sin, we deceive ourselves, and the truth is not in us" (BSB).

Awareness is key to recovery. You cannot change areas of addiction in your life if you are not aware of the problem. Much of my own awareness has come about through safe relationships in which I am able to interact honestly and be transparent. It is so helpful to have others alongside you as you explore the origin and other roots as well as what draws you back to your addictions. In his book *Unwanted: How Sexual Brokenness Reveals Our Way to Healing*, Jay Stringer wrote, "If you want to understand why you are addicted to something, you have to understand the conditions that keep your addiction in place."[20]

Through awareness of my childhood trauma, I learned the harsh story of my life. Though it may sound counterintuitive, part of the healing process for me has been learning what that story was, embracing it, then moving forward by changing the narrative of my life.

Changing your narrative is vital. First, you must understand the hold of your old narrative: the child who was abused and traumatized. Second, you move toward a new narrative, a present-day narrative that reflects how you want life to be.

BETTER TOGETHER THAN SOLO

One important aspect of trauma resolution and recovery for me is co-regulation. You might say co-regulation is a technical way of describing a soothing balm for our emotions when we work together. Put more simply, co-regulation is when people help regulate one another emotionally. The following story about a boy we'll call Drew illustrates what I am talking about:

Debbie and I walked into the church nursery on Sunday morning for our turn to serve. I was drawn to a young boy who was crying and upset, obviously missing his mom, who had checked him into the nursery so she could attend the service. I decided to sit by Drew.

My plan was not to talk him out of his current emotional state, but to listen, to hear his concerns, and to be there for him. I told Drew I wasn't leaving his side until his mom came to pick him up. He said over and over again that he missed his mom.

After a long time of crying, which got worse before it got better, he started talking. I listened to Drew as he shared that it was his birthday and he was going to have a cake with lots of sprinkles. He then shared how many sisters and brothers he had, even telling me who was the oldest and the youngest in his family.

Then, in a light moment and in a way only children can articulate, Drew shared some information about his parents' marriage. I found myself listening attentively. As tears began to flow down his little face again, I reaffirmed to Drew that I would stay with him until his mom returned. I wasn't going anywhere.

He nodded in agreement with the plan. My words of assurance seemed to comfort him, and his body began to relax. I told him I was glad I met him and was able to spend time getting to know him.

At the end of our time together, Drew asked if we could be friends. In fact, he even asked if I would come to his birthday party. We connected!

To me, that is a snapshot of co-regulation and trauma work.

One of the things I realized early in my recovery journey, something that still holds true for me today, is the healing power of being with other people who struggle with some of the same things I do. There's something so encouraging, comforting, and even magical in hearing another person say to you, "Yeah, I know. I can totally relate to that."

This isn't a new concept. The Bible gives great instruction on the need not to fly solo in our lives, especially when we have trials, problems, and burdens that need the healing touch of God. Galatians 6:2 says, "Bear one another's burdens, and so fulfill the law of Christ" (ESV). Sharing our stories—the good, the bad, and the ugly—is also a concept in Scripture. James 5:16 says, "Therefore confess your sins to each other and pray for each other so that you may be healed. The prayer of a righteous person is powerful and effective."

When you share your struggles—whether it's anxiety,

depression, addictions, triggers, or something else—with someone who can relate to you, it's a powerful connection that helps to take away the shame. Isolation exaggerates the shame. It makes you believe there is something dreadfully wrong with you because it seems like you are the only one in the world who has this problem. Something powerful happens when somebody comes alongside you and says, "Yeah, I know what that's like. I struggle with the same things."

RENEGOTIATING MY TRAUMA AND ITS EFFECTS

Trauma creates a warzone in your body. As I mentioned previously, the battle is not "one and done." You're still in the warzone years after the trauma occurred, and you react to it by either becoming hypervigilant (getting lost in a frenzy of activity or addictions to escape) or shutting down and withdrawing from a big portion of life. I've done both!

In recovery, I learned that I needed to work through my childhood trauma by renegotiating it and the effects it has had on my life. Since my trauma occurred in childhood, I experienced the trauma with a child's mind. But now, as an adult, I need to look at my traumatic experiences with adult eyes and renegotiate my response to them.

Curt Thompson, a Christian psychiatrist, states in his book *Anatomy of the Soul*, "Even though you cannot change the events of your story, you can change the way you experience your story."[21]

The Bathtub

Throughout my childhood, my mom recounted a story to me about a bath. The original incident took place when I was around two years old. My parents went to Florida for a month and left me in the care of my aunt and uncle. After my parents returned from their trip, they had problems getting me into the bathtub to give me a bath. When my mom retold this story, she explained that my aunt had put me into too hot of a bath, and I had been scalded. Now, I have no cognitive memory of this experience to which my mom repeatedly referred. However, I experienced trauma from being told the story time and again.

I tell this story because not all trauma comes solely from our direct experiences. It can also come from what we are told about ourselves. Whether it's a story, abusive words, the constant bombardment of our minds with horrific tales of crimes against humanity, or the twenty-four-hour news cycles highlighting the evil that's in the world, research shows that all these things traumatize people.

To add a layer of complexity to my bath story, my mom never said that my aunt told her I was burned in the bathtub. I'm not sure if my aunt told her anything or if my mom just assumed that's what happened. Often that's how trauma works. You don't always know exactly what happened, but you know something happened.

At the height of my addictions, I avoided taking baths, among many other things. Just thinking about taking a bath caused overwhelming fear and anxiety. Your body really does remember the trauma.

Now, having been in recovery for over seven years, I find myself taking a bath daily! Through renegotiating the trauma, taking a bath is no longer a trigger, but a practice that relaxes me and regulates my emotions. It brings calm.

My Struggle with Reading

When I was six years old, I came home from school and told my dad that I was having problems reading and my teacher said I needed some extra help. He exploded in anger and screamed at me, "Are you acting like a baby again?"

My mom arranged special tutoring for me, and the tutor gave me a simple book to take home and read. I decided to memorize it so that when I went back for my next tutoring appointment, I could recite the book to her. And that's exactly what I did. I didn't technically read the pages to her; I recited them from memory. It was my way, even as a child, to guard against making mistakes and protect myself from criticism.

Now, as an adult looking back on this difficulty, I believe it was the pivotal moment in my life when I decided never to ask for help or show vulnerability. To this day, I struggle with reading, especially reading out loud, but now I know why.

A Painful Comparison

As I've mentioned before, my dad often compared me to my cognitively challenged uncle. Since it was a different time, he would sometimes use the term "retarded" when referring to his brother. While he never directly called me retarded, he did compare me with my uncle. Imagine being a child and having your own father compare you to your uncle, whom you knew he referred to as "retarded." Whenever I took initiative to do challenging things, had different ideas, or simply had a different opinion from his, it was met with my dad's response of: "What the hell's the matter with you? Are you a goddamn fool?"

As an adult looking back on my dad's abusive words—words that made it clear my father thought I was dumb, mentally impaired, and a fool at best—I realize I compensated for those judgments by earning my bachelor's degree, then my master's, then a second master's, and finally a doctorate. Inside me, there was a powerful urge to prove him wrong.

But my educational and intellectual accomplishments and accolades, as good as they are, didn't compensate for my feelings. Though physical trauma is devastating and leaves scars, words that diminish who you are as a person cause trauma that pierces your soul.

The Roles of My Siblings and Me

When I was a child, I was never quite sure if my siblings experienced the same abuses I did. No doubt, all three of us were traumatized in different ways. From my perspective, each of us played a different role in our family.

My brother was the hero; he was up on a pedestal. He was named after our dad and was the namesake of the family.

Later in life, he followed in the footsteps of my dad in the construction business. He worked with our dad's company and eventually took it over as our dad got older. Sadly, my brother passed a few years ago.

My sister was the forgotten child. She was vastly ignored by my parents, which in and of itself, can be a form of abuse or trauma.

I was the scapegoat. Much of the outward abuse was directed toward me.

Everybody in a family sees the family differently. Each person has a different story to tell. Dr. Curt Thompson described this idea perfectly when he wrote, "No sibling grows up in the same household."[22]

It's like a car crash with various eyewitnesses. Each person who witnessed the accident will tell a different version of what happened. All of the different stories are accurate because the witnesses were standing in different positions that provided different points of view.

There is no doubt that my siblings experienced trauma. I want to acknowledge that here in my book. At the same time, I'm choosing not to give detailed information about what I know of their experiences in our family. My sister's story is her story, not mine. My brother's story was his story, not mine (and that doesn't change now that he has passed on).

NEVER ALONE: GOD HAS GUIDED ME EVERY STEP OF THE WAY

There is no doubt in my mind that God has been guiding me in this process of facing my addictions, going to rehab, and walking through recovery. In fact, I now know the Lord has always been with me, even when I wasn't aware of it.

Second Timothy 2:13 says, "If we are faithless, He remains faithful; He cannot deny Himself" (NKJV). I had stopped going to church for quite some time during my addictions. Earlier in my adult life, I heard teachings that told me simply to trust and obey God. If I do that, everything will be okay. It is important to trust and obey God, but for those who have suffered trauma, abuse, or other types of horrific experiences, healing is not as simple as some in church make it seem. They are well-intentioned, don't get me wrong, but the oversimplification can often cause trauma sufferers not to feel safe in a church environment.

I go to church regularly now and not only feel safe, but also encouraged. I enjoy the fellowship of other believers. I learned in rehab that God was pursuing me because He loved me. He came to me in kindness, not in judgement, and it is the kindness of God that leads to change.

It's okay for me to feel depressed. It's okay for me to experience anxiety. It's okay for me to encounter discouragement. And it's okay for me to have flashbacks, as painful as they are. I am learning that I can be real with God about all these things. I once felt I needed to get my act together before God could love me, but God loves us in our messes. He loves us enough to lead us through our trials, our hurts, and our brokenness.

Because of God's kindness and love, I have learned to be kinder and more compassionate about my life. He taught me that I didn't have to take a sledgehammer to myself or to my story. Instead of beating myself up all day for feeling one way or another or struggling with this thought or that thought, I'm learning to have more compassion for myself and more empathy for others.

I want to assure you that God loves you just as you are. He is not overwhelmed by your story, your addictions, or your trauma. In fact, He knows your story better than you know it, and He can guide you through your healing journey, every step of the way.

I'm amazed, day in and day out, how God shows up and uses me in ways I never believed were possible. Being able to work with others who have been traumatized and see them come alive on their healing journeys—to me, that's a joy like no other. And to see first-time clients come in to see me, doubled over with shame, hiding their pills, struggling with addictions, and trying to escape their stories, and to be able to offer them hope, compassion, and the glorious words: "Yeah, I know. I can relate"—that, too, is a gift from God.

The Lord is sending me people who are struggling in the same areas I've struggled, and they are able to receive from me grace, compassion, and empathy. Second Corinthians 1:3–4 says, "Praise be to the God and Father of our Lord Jesus Christ, the Father of compassion and the God of all comfort, who comforts us in all our troubles, so that we can comfort those in any trouble with the comfort we ourselves receive from God."

I thought I had to get my act together to be loved by God, but day in and day out, God runs to me, like He did to the prodigal son, offering a platter of compassion, acceptance, and grace. His message to me is: "Come, My son, and rest and heal. Experience My love. You are My beloved."

For me, deep healing, while painful, offers a new beginning for transformation. When I can experience pain, anger, shame, guilt, sadness, and repentance, it provides fresh opportunities to see the hope of God's redemption. I may initially greet these kinds of opportunities for growth with great resistance, but if I am patient with myself and the process, allowing change somehow brings forth gratitude.

Chapter Eight Reflections

Question: What are some ways, big or small, you see God at work in your healing process? As you are learning your story, are there insights or opportunities opening to you?

____

____

____

____

____

____

____

____

____

Question: What is your old narrative? What is the new narrative you want to move toward? In what areas of your life would you like to pursue healing?

Question: Is there a message you believe God is revealing to you?

Chapter Eight Notes

CHAPTER NINE

Grace Gets the Last Word

God invites us into a story where grace gets the last word.[23]

—Pastor Nate Davis

If you had asked me ten years ago to draw a picture of my life, I think I would have asked for a small, blank piece of paper with a black crayon. But if you were to ask me today, I would want a big, white poster board and a 120-crayon Crayola box! That's how different my life is today.

God Meets Us in the Messiness of Life

God knows my story, and He knows yours. For too many decades, I thought I needed to clean up my act to be loved by God. But when I was in rehab, I started to realize God loved me in my messiness. That's who He is, a God who meets us in the messiness of our lives with kindness, love, and grace. I have experienced His grace time and again.

As a child, I never felt accepted by God, just as I never felt accepted by my parents. They never showed me grace. My weaknesses were not only used against me, but were held up as a reason to withhold love from me. In fact, I was unaware I was even lovable.

However, God vanquished those lies I had learned to believe. He said, "I have loved you with an everlasting love; I have drawn you with unfailing kindness" (Jeremiah 31:3). That is what He says to you, too. Right there in your messiness. Right there in your brokenness. Right there in your sins.

This acceptance from God when I was at the beginning of my messy journey spurred me on throughout the difficult, painful process as I took each step toward healing. Anyone who's participated in recovery knows it's not a procedure, but a process. It's an ongoing, daily, living process!

I spent years of my life overwhelmed by my weaknesses and my failures. I learned growing up not to show my vulnerabilities or hurts. I became good at hiding. But my faith allows me not only to explore the areas of weakness in my life, but to accept them. It was a revelation to me that I could embrace my weakness with joy.

Second Corinthians 12:9–11 says, "But he said to me, 'My grace is sufficient for you, for my power is made perfect in weakness.' Therefore I will boast all the more gladly about my weaknesses, so that Christ's power may rest on me. That is why, for Christ's sake, I delight in weaknesses, in insults, in hardships, in persecutions, in difficulties. For when I am weak, then I am strong."

DON'T GO IT ALONE: THE IMPORTANCE OF THE "ONE ANOTHERS"

We were created to live in community, yet those who have experienced trauma or addiction gravitate toward isolation. Prior to going to rehab, I had gotten to a point where I didn't want to be around anybody. I stopped going to work. I spent much of my day in bed or watching TV. I no longer wanted to be around friends. I didn't go with my wife and daughter to see family on Thanksgiving or Christmas. Instead, I chose to stay home alone. My marriage suffered, my relationship with my daughter suffered, and I was miserable.

As I shared in earlier chapters about rehab, I was not one who wanted to join group counseling sessions. I didn't want to share my story with anyone. If left to my own choices, I gladly would have spent a lot of time by myself in my room at rehab. But they didn't allow much time alone at all. There's a reason for that: isolation is not a part of the healing process.

Sharing our stories with others who are safe and can relate to what we've been through is a means of catharsis. My recovery process includes other people! Just as I developed friendships in rehab that ended up being a huge encouragement on my journey forward, so, too, in recovery, I started working with a group of men who had experiences similar to mine.

I also learned in recovery that I need flesh and bones when it comes to love. I need people to show it to me. As a child, I didn't receive that kind of love. But as I opened up to others while at rehab and then followed up with my group in recovery, I realized just how much we need one another in life.

God created us to need one another. We are not meant to be islands, but rather functioning parts of a community. Jesus said, "'Love the Lord your God with all your heart and with all your soul and with all your mind.' This is the first and greatest commandment. And the second is like it: 'Love your neighbor as yourself.' All the Law and the Prophets hang on these two commandments" (Matthew 22:37–40).

What's our purpose in life? According to Jesus, it's to love God and to love one another! Loving one another includes bearing one another's burdens and being there for each other in the good times and the bad. We are also to confess our sins to one another, which includes sharing our stories with others. I think it's worth looking at the places where the Bible uses the phrase "one another" or "each other." I've compiled some of the Scripture references that use this wording. I encourage you to study these verses as well as the many others found in Scripture. They are a snapshot of how God desires for us to be in community with others:

- "Be at peace with each other." (Mark 9:50)
- "Wash one another's feet." (John 13:14)
- "Love one another." (John 13:34)
- "Honor one another above yourselves." (Romans 12:10)
- "Live in harmony with one another." (Romans

12:16)

- "Stop passing judgment on one another." (Romans 14:13)
- "Accept one another, then, just as Christ accepted you." (Romans 15:7)
- "Instruct one another." (Romans 15:14)
- "Serve one another humbly in love." (Galatians 5:13)
- "Carry each other's burdens." (Galatians 6:2)
- "Be kind and compassionate to one another, forgiving each other." (Ephesians 4:32)
- "In humility consider others more important than yourselves." (Philippians 2:3 BSB)
- "Admonish one another." (Colossians 3:16)
- "Encourage one another and build each other up." (1 Thessalonians 5:11)
- "Confess your sins to each other." (James 5:16)
- "Pray for each other." (James 5:16)
- "Use whatever gift you have received to serve others." (1 Peter 4:10)

TWO METAPHORS FOR MY LIFE

There are two metaphors that describe my life. The first one, about dandelions, describes my life prior to rehab. Dandelions are a quick-growing and quick-spreading floral weed. They are invasive and often choke out the life of other flowers or plants in your yard. Sometimes people make the mistake of removing only the leaves and flowers without digging out the roots. Their yards will look better on the surface for a time, but because the roots were not removed, they grow more robust in the ground. Soon the plants reappear with new vitality. In fact, they come back in greater number than before.

For years, I learned to look good on the outside. I focused on how I appeared to others and did not address the root of my problems. No matter how things appeared on the outside, my destructive thoughts and behaviors continued to grow on the inside. Soon the root problems in my life grew to the point where they appeared on the outside as well.

If a gardener only lops off the tops of dandelions, it stimulates the roots to grow deeper, and then weeds appear on the surface in an even bigger way. Ignoring your problems instead of digging down deep into their roots will result in deeper pain and more destructive behaviors. Eventually, as happened with me, your inner struggles will make their way to the surface, and you will find yourself at a crossroads.

The second metaphor describes my life in recovery. I am an enthusiastic fan of Kintsugi, a special Japanese pottery. In what is known as the Kintsugi process, the potter takes a broken piece of pottery and mends it back together using pure gold.[24] The piece ends up becoming far more beautiful and valuable than it was in its original state.

God does the same thing with broken lives. Throughout recovery, God has been in the process of redeeming my brokenness—mending, molding, and conforming me to reflect the image of Jesus Christ. Isaiah 64:8 says, "Yet you, LORD, are our Father. We are the clay, you are the potter; we are all the work of your hand."

We are broken, but God comes along and puts us back together. Not only does He restore us, but if we give Him the opportunity, He will also create something much greater than we could ever imagine. Through God, I am much bigger than the addictions that used to have a hold on my life. Through God's grace, I am now becoming bigger than my story, the same story that, for most of my life, was too big for me.

We Are All Wounded and Broken

We all have been wounded and broken in life. That's because we live in a fallen world dominated by sin. The sin in the world brings about trauma, which brings about woundedness, and woundedness brings about more sin. It's a vicious cycle.

There was a lot of hurt inflicted upon me in my life, and as a result, I caused other people a lot of hurt. As they say in recovery, "hurt people hurt people." This devastating cycle of hurt can go from generation to generation unless we break it.

How do we break the cycle? Where does our help come from? One of the names for God in Hebrew is *Jehovah Rapha*, which means "God is our healer."[25] It's the Lord who heals. Christ came to earth in human form, died on the cross, and rose from the grave to break the curse of sin in our lives. By God's grace, we all can be healed and restored.

God has certainly shown up in my story. He showed up in rehab, and He continues to show up in my life every day. I can honestly say that God has transformed my life. He is all about restoration. That's what He does. He takes something that's broken and puts it back together better than it was.

My life today is a far cry from the unwanted behaviors, addictions, and withdrawal from life that I experienced ten years ago. I am not so naïve as to believe I am not going to be triggered in diverse ways the rest of my life, considering the kind of abuse I suffered as a child. But I now have tools to help me respond to those triggers so they don't impact my life. I've experienced so much healing in all areas of my life—physical, mental, relational, and, of course, spiritual. I really do look forward to getting up in the morning!

FORGIVENESS IS THE KEY

Forgiveness is the key that unlocks the prison doors of bitterness, resentment, and even hate. Lewis B. Smedes, renowned theologian and ethicist, once wrote, "To forgive is to set a prisoner free and discover that the prisoner was you."[26]

Like recovery, forgiveness is a process. As new memories

of my childhood surface or are triggered, I often find myself wrestling with emotions of anger, resentment, and bitterness. I realize my anger is a secondary emotion. It springs from fear, frustration, hurt, or a combination of all these feelings.

Addressing the issue of anger is a wide area on which I am presently working. When anger comes, it's not manifested in outward temperament or action; I internalize it. I shut down or go into hypo-arousal. It's then that I go back to my tools of either talking to somebody about it or writing everything down in my journal. These tools help me to regulate my emotions and bring about resolution.

Though my emotions are understandable, if I don't regulate them, they can fester and grab control of my heart, robbing me of the joy and peace I have in Christ. The apostle Paul wrote, "Be kind and compassionate to one another, forgiving each other, just as in Christ God forgave you" (Ephesians 4:32).

Just as I had to confess and repent of my sins before God while in rehab and then in recovery, I also had to ask many people for their forgiveness for how I hurt them, treated them, or emotionally distanced myself from them.

We forgive others because Christ forgave us. We didn't deserve forgiveness, but the Lord loved us, forgave us, and died for us "while we were still sinners" (Romans 5:8). We can forgive those who hurt us, whether they are sorry or not, because God forgave us. It's this process of forgiveness that is the key to letting go of past offenses and hurts.

As Chuck DeGroat said, "The deep work of exploring our stories is as much about seeing how we show up in the present as it is how we experienced our past. If we can only name how we've been hurt and if we cannot take responsibility for how we show up today, we've missed the real power of story work."[27]

FINDING A "WONDERFUL ENDING" IN THE PROCESS

> *...and those the LORD has rescued will return. They will enter Zion with singing; everlasting joy will crown their heads. Gladness and joy will overtake them, and sorrow and sighing will flee away.*
>
> ***—Isaiah 35:10***

"Have you recovered?"

"Are you healed now?"

"So, you are all fixed now, right?"

These are some of the questions I have been asked over the last few years. All have been asked in a sincere and often caring way—though word choices, such as "fixed," could be tweaked! They are genuine questions. It's our human nature to want wonderful endings in which everything is fixed and life is now perfect. But you know, as I do, that nothing will ever be perfect until we are in heaven.

That's why my answer to those questions is: "Recovery is a lifelong process for me. Yes, I have experienced tremendous healing. I am not addicted to medications, alcohol, or any other substance. I'm doing well. But I'm not done with my recovery process. In fact, God's restoration and transformation process is still a work in progress and will continue throughout my lifetime!"

I have come a long way since entering rehab, and in so many ways, my life today is drastically different from what it was ten years ago. But I do still get triggers, and I still have things that need changing. Maybe you are thinking right now, *"Wow, Mark, that's deflating. There's no wonderful ending!"* I have good news for you: there is plenty of wonderful in this journey of recovery and transformation. There is now immense joy in my life, no matter how I feel or what circumstances come my way, and there is peace. I actually experience serenity!

As a Christian, I am continually growing, transforming, and being molded and shaped into the person God wants me to be. And that, dear friend, is a lifelong process, so be encouraged! There is healing, restoration, and *life* at the end of the tunnel if you take the time to start walking through that process—one step at a time, one foot after the other.

When I finished rehab seven years ago, I remember looking around and, with great fear and trepidation, thinking, *"Now what, Lord?"*

I was afraid of what was coming next, the challenging work of recovery and the unknowns of the future.

Now I wake up in the morning with joy in my heart. Now, instead of fear and trepidation, I'm excited about life and what each day holds.

I encourage you, friend, to take that step toward healing. It's worth it. Don't do it alone. Reach out to a counselor, get help with your addiction, and find a safe person and community to share your story with.

Most importantly, know that God loves you and accepts you just as you are, right there in the messiness of your life. He is pursuing you, so open the door of your life to Him. You will never regret doing so.

Jesus said, "The thief comes only to steal and kill and destroy. I came that they may have life and have it abundantly" (John 10:10 ESV).

I close this book in the same way I started this journey, but this time in anticipation of what is next on the horizon: *"Now what, Lord?"*

Chapter Nine Reflections

Question: Do you gravitate toward isolation or struggle to connect in community? What steps can you take to be more engaged in a loving, encouraging community?

____

____

____

____

____

____

____

____

____

Question: Are you addressing the surface appearance of your inner struggles instead of the root of the problem? How can you start addressing the root?

Question: Whom do you need to pursue forgiving as a part of your healing process? Do you need to forgive yourself as well? Do you have resentment toward God you need to release?

Chapter Nine Notes

Acknowledgments

To my Lord and Savior, Jesus Christ—You've never given up on me. You saved me from my sin. You encourage me to pursue wholeness daily. You accept me as I am, to help me become who I am meant to be.

Debbie—thank you for standing by me and encouraging me on this journey, and for your unwavering faith in God. Thanks, too, for reading this manuscript what seems like one million times. I love you!

Emily and Brandon—thanks for your support, encouragement, and love. You make me smile. I am so proud of you. I love you both!

Harry Flanagan—words cannot begin to express my gratitude for you. This book would not be if it weren't for you. Thank you for the grace you demonstrate every time we speak.

"Brennan"—thanks for showing up in my life. You have been a God-send on so many levels. Your ongoing friendship means so much to me.

Jack and Eva Kroeze—thank you for having the vision to encourage me to write my story down as a book.

Tyler Minton—my friend on the "other side of the

world" (well, actually, Washington state). Thank you for your input, support, wisdom, and prayers. I'm so grateful for you and your friendship!

The guys in my Tuesday night group—thank you for being there, accepting me, and teaching me what recovery looks like.

Celeste Jacque—thank you for being a lifelong friend who has always been there through my ups and downs.

Leslie Bayles—your gentleness and kindness have been essential to my recovery.

Dr. Garbley—your knowledge and kindness came at just the right time.

Jay Stringer—I'm grateful for you. I appreciate your skills that have allowed me to understand the depth of my intricate and complex story.

Thank you to everyone who has read the manuscript and provided encouragement and input. And thanks to Caleb Breakey and the Team at Renown Publishing—I couldn't have done this without you!

About the Author

Dr. Mark M. McNear is a Licensed Clinical Social Worker and maintains a private practice in New Jersey. With over thirty years of experience in clinical practice, Dr. McNear now focuses on helping those who have had trauma and abuse in their lives, sharing the hope of healing that he has personally experienced for himself. He is a graduate of Northeastern Bible College, New York University, and Oxford Graduate School. Dr. McNear is also a popular speaker, a frequent guest on nationally syndicated radio broadcasts, an author, and a featured panelist in several videos dealing with Christianity and mental health.

About Renown Publishing

Renown Publishing was founded with one mission in mind: to make your great idea famous.

At Renown Publishing, we don't just publish. We work hard to pair strategy with innovative marketing techniques so that your book launch is the start of something bigger.

Learn more at RenownPublishing.com.

Notes

1. Manning, Brennan. *The Ragamuffin Gospel: Good News for the Bedraggled, Beat-Up, and Burnt Out*. Crown Publishing Group, 2008, p. 25.

2. van der Kolk, Bessel. *The Body Keeps the Score: Brain, Mind, and Body in the Healing of Trauma*. Penguin Publishing Group, 2015.

3. Rohr, Richard. "Transforming Pain." Center for Action and Contemplation. October 17, 2018. https://cac.org/transforming-pain-2018-10-17/.

4. Maté, Gabor. "Beyond Drugs: The Universal Experience of Addiction." April 5, 2017. https://drgabormate.com/opioids-universal-experience-addiction/.

5. Fisher, Janina. *Transforming the Living Legacy of Trauma: A Workbook for Survivors and Therapists*. PESI, 2021.

6. Black, Claudia. *It Will Never Happen to Me: Growing Up with Addiction as Youngsters, Adolescents, Adults.* Hazelden Publishing, 2009.

7. Condusiv Technologies. "What Is Defragmentation and Why Do I Need It?" https://condusiv.com/disk-defrag/defragmentation/.

8. Minton, Tyler. "I was unfaithful in my marriage." Facebook, September 21, 2021. https://www.facebook.com/tminton33/posts/10159675213474661?__cft__[0]=AZWYgwdOv5HBUia6ZPkVgrxUOAvVYDItSYrUpz1bYKhhIULRJY2mJ2fMn-LDD3BK4uNUDcvOj7EtPPjtjoA3_69Eec32kWKMeGHjrDULRdY1i54mjJ85JgqDoFx5RZvzTVkLeel-HqHrLUYs8tv2E5M0B-wyJuNFev-O29FIJ6qRBw&__tn__=%2CO%2CP-R.

9. Pelzer, Dave. *A Child Called It: One Child's Courage to Survive.* Health Communications, Incorporated, 1995, p.166.

10. van der Kolk, *The Body Keeps the Score.*

11. Davis, Laura. *Allies in Healing: When the Person You Love Was Sexually Abused as a Child.* HarperCollins, 2012.

12. Black, *It Will Never Happen to Me.*

13. Hamilton, Laurell K. *Mistral's Kiss.* Ballantine Books, 2006, p.169.

14. Langberg, Diane. *Suffering and the Heart of God: How Trauma Destroys and Christ Restores.* New Growth Press, 2015.

15. Padre. "Understanding Your Story—An Interview with Dan Allender." And Sons Magazine, 2014. https://archive.andsonsmagazine.com/07/understanding-your-story-interview-dan-allender.

16. Yancey, P., A. Sorenson, and S. Sorenson. *Vanishing Grace Study Guide: Whatever Happened to the Good News?* Zondervan, 2014.

17. Roberts, Ted. *7 Pillars of Freedom Workbook.* Pure Desire Ministries International, 2021.

18. Warren, Rick. *The Purpose Driven Life: What on Earth Am I Here For?* Zondervan, 2002, p. 28.

19. Online Etymology Dictionary, "trauma." https://www.etymonline.com/word/trauma.

20. Stringer, Jay. *Unwanted: How Sexual Brokenness Reveals Our Way to Healing*. The Navigators, (n.d.).

21. Thompson, Curt. *Anatomy of the Soul: Surprising Connections Between Neuroscience and Spiritual Practices That Can Transform Your Life and Relationships*. Tyndale House Publishers, 2010.

22. Thompson, *Anatomy of the Soul*.

23. Davis, Nate. "Moving Toward Forgiveness." Christ Community Church, July 10, 2021. YouTube video. https://www.youtube.com/watch?v=6hV5aBfBU0A.

24. Sho, Terushi. "Kintsugi: Japan's Ancient Art of Embracing Imperfection." BBC. January 8, 2021. https://www.bbc.com/travel/article/20210107-kintsugi-japans-ancient-art-of-embracing-imperfection.

25. Bentorah, Chaim. *Hebrew Word Study: Revealing the Heart of God*. Whitaker House, 2016.

26. Smedes, Lewis B. *Forgive and Forget: Healing the Hurts We Don't Deserve*. HarperCollins, 1996.

27. DeGroat, Chuck. "The deep work of exploring our stories is as much about seeing how we show up in the present as it is how we experienced our past." May 28, 2021. https://www.facebook.com/photo/?fbid=10161527889955329&set=a.10150408198285329.

Made in the USA
Middletown, DE
09 April 2024